T0339694

Media, Central American Refugees, and the U.S. Border Crisis

This book identifies the history, conventions, and uses of security discourses, and argues that such language and media frames distort information and mislead the public, misidentify the focus of concern, and omit narratives able to recognize the causes and solutions to humanitarian crises.

What has been identified as a crisis at the border is better understood as an on-going crisis of violence, building over decades, that has forced migrants from their homes in the countries of the Northern Triangle. Authors Robin Andersen and Adrian Bergmann look back to U.S. military policies in the region and connect this legacy to the cross-border development of transnational gangs, government corruption, and on-going violence that often targets environmental and legal defenders. They argue that the discourses of demonization and securitization only help perpetuate brutality in both Central America and the United States, especially in the desert borderlands of the southwest. They offer ways in which stories of migrants can be reframed within the language of justice, empathy, and humanitarianism.

A compelling examination of language, media, and politics, this book is both highly contemporary and widely applicable, perfect for students and scholars of global media, political communications, and their many intersections.

Robin Andersen is Professor of Communication and Media Studies at Fordham University. She is the author of seven books and dozens of book chapters and journal articles, and writes media analysis and criticism for a variety of publications. She co-edited the *Routledge Companion to Media and Humanitarian Action*, and she is now editing the Routledge Focus on Media and Humanitarian Action series. She also recently published *HBO's* Treme *and the Stories of the Storm: From New Orleans as Disaster Myth to Groundbreaking*

Television. Her 2006 book *A Century of Media: A Century of War* won the 2007 Alpha Sigma Nu Book Award from the Honor Society of Jesuit Colleges and Universities. She is a Project Censored Judge, and her article for Fairness and Accuracy in Reporting was recognized as a Top Ten Story for 2018.

Adrian Bergmann is a Research Fellow at the Institute of Historical, Anthropological, and Archaeological Studies of the University of El Salvador, where he conducts interdisciplinary research on peace building, conflict transformation, and violence reduction. Previously, he held the Chair of Peace Culture at Don Bosco University, and he has worked as a scholar and practitioner with street children, sex workers, gang members, police officers, and policy-makers. At present, he is focused on the transformation of dynamics of armed violence, the role of the state in the production of violence, and strategies for constructive engagement with gangs.

Routledge Focus on Media and Humanitarian Action

Robin Andersen and Purnaka L. de Silva

Humanitarianism is defined by assumptions that guide global solidarity, and posits that all peoples are part of the same humanity, no matter who they are, what they believe or where they live. These principles suggest that when media show the suffering of others, global publics respond in ways that facilitate disaster relief and help alleviate pain. But reactions to crises are also shaped by those who bear witness, tell the stories, share the data, and take the pictures of communities rocked by crises. Media content can also help those humanitarians who seek to address root causes of disasters, or it can serve to obscure the causes in many ways.

This series explores the multiple intersections between media and the work of humanitarian actors, and offers critical analysis of media, its uses, its coverage, how it has changed, and how it is misused in the representation of humanitarianism. Authors identify cutting-edge uses of new media technologies, including big data and virtual reality, and assess the conventions of older legacy media. For movements toward global peace, all peoples should be represented at the table and have their voices heard, including those outside the media spotlight.

Media, Central American Refugees, and the U.S. Border Crisis
Security Discourses, Immigrant Demonization, and the
Perpetuation of Violence
Robin Andersen and Adrian Bergmann

For more information about this series visit: https://www.routledge.com/Routledge-Focus-on-Media-and-Humanitarian-Action/book-series/RFMHA

Media, Central American Refugees, and the U.S. Border Crisis

Security Discourses, Immigrant Demonization, and the Perpetuation of Violence

Robin Andersen and Adrian Bergmann

Routledge
Taylor & Francis Group

NEW YORK AND LONDON

First published 2020
by Routledge
52 Vanderbilt Avenue, New York, NY 10017

and by Routledge
2 Park Square, Milton Park, Abingdon, Oxon, OX14 4RN

Routledge is an imprint of the Taylor & Francis Group, an informa business

First issued in paperback 2021

Library of Congress Cataloging-in-Publication Data
A catalog record for this title has been requested

ISBN: 978-0-367-18971-6 (hbk)
ISBN: 978-1-03-209201-0 (pbk)
ISBN: 978-0-429-19959-2 (ebk)

Typeset in Times New Roman
by codeMantra

For the Migrants of the Northern Triangle, El Salvador, Honduras, and Guatemala forced to leave their homes.

Contents

Preface

Robin Andersen

The authors of this volume have been for years deeply involved in the topics presented here. Each has been on-the-ground, so to speak, in Central America, and their observations and analysis are bolstered by personal experiences. Many times those experiences have been troubling but have caused each to care deeply about the people caught in the destructive forces detailed here.

As a young graduate student studying the newsgathering practices of U.S. journalists, I followed a freelance news crew to El Salvador in the late fall and early spring of 1979–1980. My friend John Hoagland was working as a sound-tech for the news crew. He made the arrangements that allowed me to follow him and his colleagues, Carl and Kathy, in El Salvador. I watched as they, often bravely in the face of personal danger, gathered the elements they needed to construct TV news stories. Sometimes editors in the States would add footage that the crew had not shot or included in their visual feeds.

It was a period of mass demonstrations against a repressive regime that had just come to power promising reform. At that time, El Salvador was on the brink of civil war, yet there remained some small hope that change might occur without armed conflict. Over the time I was there, that political opening closed. I watched as peaceful demonstrators were attacked by military forces and paramilitary snipers.

Covering one demonstration, I broke from the crew and ran along the line of organizers, asking them questions about why they were in the street and what their demands were. A young woman passed me a colored pompom made of paper, similar to the ones cheerleaders wave at sports events. When I found the crew again, they saw the pompom and become very agitated, telling me all at once in alarmed tones: *Get that out of your pocket. It makes you a target. See those rifles on the rooftops? Don't give them an excuse to shoot you, or us!* Kathy, who was the on-air reporter, had caught a bullet in the arm a few weeks earlier, and her arm was still bandaged. We were all well aware that the threat came from security forces, not leftist organizers.

One day we entered a compound on the outskirts of the city in a wealthy neighborhood where houses were surrounded by tall fences. Guards toting semi-automatic rifles observed us with suspicion as they ushered us through the gate. In the courtyard, sitting behind a table, was a mild-mannered-looking man whose large, melancholy eyes were belied by his baleful gaze. He was Roberto D'Aubuisson, leader of one of the paramilitary death squads about to unleash a wave of terror on the people of El Salvador. His handler, a man who had been trained at Massachusetts Institute of Technology (MIT), listened intently to Carl and Kathy's questions, cutting them off occasionally if the query was too direct.

A little later we covered a priest preforming a Catholic service at a large, opulent church in San Salvador. Leaving the church through the tall wooden doors that opened onto the city, the priest of small stature offered me his hand, and his charismatic presence was overwhelming. He was the Archbishop Oscar Arnulfo Romero, and a few weeks later he would be assassinated by a paramilitary death squad, now openly operating in the city. Journalist Raymond Bonner would later report that Roberto D'Aubuisson's operation was responsible for killing the Archbishop.[1]

When I returned to my university, I was shocked to see the way news reports covered events I had experienced in El Salvador at the time. Over the course of years, those reports did not get much better. The representations bore little resemblance to the political forces and military violence I had seen gaining a stronghold in the country. Most importantly, I was deeply affected by the people of El Salvador, their generosity, and their courage. John would frequently marvel at how nice the people were, and one day, pointing to a row of cars along the street, he noted that few had locked doors. Many had their windows open. He remarked how safe the city was. That, of course, was about to change, and as the United States supported the forces of brutality, the country would never be the same again. John later became a photojournalist working for *Newsweek* magazine in war zones around the world. He was killed in 1984 covering the conflict in El Salvador, "caught in crossfire." At age 36, he became the tenth foreign journalist to be killed covering the U.S.-backed civil war.

El Salvador would change dramatically over the course of the war, and the region would be transformed by the twenty-first century to one of the most dangerous places on the globe. I would dedicate much of my academic career to trying to understand and explain how and why such violence was unleashed in the region and identify the forces that did, and still do, so much harm to the people there. The Central American migrants today, characterized as an invading force by the 45th President, are refugees fleeing the violence that now engulfs their countries. I am deeply committed to the notion that we must come to terms with the history of U.S. involvement in this brutality as a first step to finding ways to restore and reconstruct the institutions necessary to make those counties livable again. Only then will the forced migrations of the people of the Northern Triangle, in El Salvador, Honduras, and Guatemala, come to an end.

Our hope is that this volume—by reminding us to remember these histories and offering an understanding of the dynamics that cause humanitarian crises—can, in some small way, help find a pathway to end the cycles of violence and conflict that perpetuate human suffering across the Americas.

Note

1 Raymond Bonner, "Time for a US Apology for El Salvador," *The Nation*, April 15, 2016, www.thenation.com/article/time-for-a-us-apology-to-el-salvador/

Introduction

Robin Andersen

In the late fall of 2018, as Central American migrants headed for the United States, they traveled together through Guatemala and Mexico to ensure their own safety. Over the years, migrants have become targets, increasingly exposed to exploitation, attacks, and violence on what is a very dangerous journey.[1] For weeks, as they headed northward, the 45th President of the United States used campaign rallies and social media to demonize the men, women and children forced to leave their home countries wracked by violence. Guatemala, Honduras, and El Salvador are now known as the Northern Triangle, a designation that identifies the region as one of the most dangerous places on the globe. Leading up to the mid-term elections held in November, the U.S. President identified himself at one rally as a "nationalist," adding rhetorical, unfounded flourishes asserting that America was under attack by criminals, drug dealers, and terrorists, saying "what's happening now…is an assault on our country." In increasingly sensationalistic terms, news media repeated the language of "invasion," which quickly solidified into an interpretive news framework. Press reports followed the President's lead, often augmenting it with their own invasion lexicon. ABC News called the situation a "caravan crisis," and the Associated Press invoked a "marching army," saying, "A ragged, growing army of migrants resumes march toward U.S." As *Deconstructed* noted, "If media is to be believed, the United States is about to be overrun by a horde of terrorists and criminals from Central America. And it's not just Fox News or Breitbart that are partaking in this narrative."[2]

Throughout the 2016 electoral campaign, candidate Trump labeled undocumented Mexican immigrants "rapists" and "criminals," and promised his supporters he would build a "big beautiful" border wall. Over the course of his presidency, Trump frequently reprised the winning rhetoric of xenophobia and used it again as a major campaign theme during the 2018 mid-term elections. His assiduously rehearsed narrative, threatening that an invasion would take place at the border, was frequently repeated in the press. Yet even as the electorate rebuked the President and his party, evidenced by a democratic sweep when the dust of the elections settled, media repeated the language and clung to the militarized themes and phrases of "security discourses" that dominated coverage.

Such security discourses that frame media coverage run long and deep in American culture and politics, and have been employed over the years to justify and interpret American Foreign Policy toward Central and South America. This may be best illustrated by comparing the words of Donald Trump to those of Ronald Reagan, who, in a TV address in June of 1983, warned that unless a tough stand was taken against communism in Nicaragua, "a 'tidal wave' of 'feetpeople' would be 'swarming into our country.'" Reagan used the threat of an invasion from a "migrant horde" to justify crushing leftist movements in Central America. Only through military intervention, he proclaimed, could such a "flood be stopped."[3]

A quarter of a century later, the "threats of invasion" from Central Americans continue to serve political policy goals, most notably those of Donald Trump and the U.S. military. But even before Trump announced his presidential run, the online website Breitbart, and other alt-right sites, had joined Fox News with stories about immigrants "overrunning" the southern boarders of the United States. As Adrian Bergmann writes in these pages, Breitbart warned that "thousands of illegal immigrants have overrun U.S. border security and their processing centers in Texas along the U.S./Mexico border,"[4] forging a shift in policy orientation—especially among Republican lawmakers—from immigration reform to fighting against immigration.[5] We find that in the twenty-first century, the consequences of security discourses are considerable. They help shape media coverage and sway public opinion, and are particularly influential when used by politicians. Most importantly, they serve the desires of those who would rule by force as they help shape and are shaped by policies based in militarism. As we will argue in these pages, security discourses perpetrate violence historically and currently remain the dominant discursive force helping shape American Foreign Policy. Also apparent in media images, faint though clearly visible, is another media frame and another point of view—an alternative narrative for global peace and stability, one developed over the later decades of the twentieth century based on humanitarian inclusivity. We hope this book brings those visions into clearer focus and offers its readers a definitively argued choice between violence and brutality, and a more humane view of the world, one based on the principles of human rights, dignity, and equality.

Security Discourses

The language used to frame Central American immigrants as threats to American security can be identified as part of a dangerously preemptive discourse that shapes news coverage through a set of militarized parameters. Once a security discourse is engaged, it quickly defines the terms of media debate, directing what will and will not be covered, what information can be included, and what must be left out. According to media theorist Robert Entman, framing "essentially involves selection and salience."[6] Frames "help" readers interpret what is and what is not important, frequently offering meaning through structural implication. Gamson points out that a frame is a "central organizing" principle that directs the text to focus on "what is at issue."[7] By ordering particular themes with others, media promote a problem/solution logic that leads the public to favor one interpretation over another.[8]

The logic of security stems from a set of fundamental assumptions that the world and its people are dangerous and unequal, a world where humanity is divided between us and them, and where the foreigner cannot be embraced as a member of our own community. As such, migrants are inherently undeserving of our generosity because they are not and can never be like us. Dehumanized as enemies to be feared, there is no discursive space for the migrant story to be told. They are unidimensional, foreign, alien, and "othered." Security discourses block humanitarian frames that present all people, especially those who suffer, as equal and deserving of dignity and protection. Yet it was Eleanor Roosevelt as the First Lady of the United States who nurtured and supported the Universal Declaration of Human Rights,[9] a document and global attitude that recently celebrated seven decades of established and recognized principles.

Framed within the language of security, migrants easily lose any claim that they might have had to be treated with compassion. After all, they are criminals, gang members, murderers, and rapists. This process of linguistic "othering" demonizes and dehumanizes migrants. "Othered" in this way, migrants can only pose a threat to nationalist goals. When they arrive at our borders, they are "illegal aliens," a phrase that quickly strips them of their humanity. Claims to be treated with justice and dignity are not recognized because refugees now exist in the twilight of criminality, waiting to coalesce as an invading force, an enemy.

Once identified as dangerous, the narrative then follows a proscribed pattern. Actions against the invaders must be taken to protect us from them. At this point, any means of stopping the "feetpeople," or "migrant hordes" from "invading, "swarming," and "flooding" into our country can be applied. The story then turns to the military response.

After Trump announced that he would send U.S. soldiers to meet the migrants at the border, media covered troop deployments and movements, interviewing those who could offer "expert military analysis," often presented by former and current members of the armed forces. Media coverage about the migrants followed Trump's lead, even as military deployment in domestic affairs violates the U.S. constitution. Focusing on border security, discussions then revolved around weaponry and justifications for the use of force. As the story progressed, opportunities to offer context for the migration or answer questions about the migrants themselves or the reasons for their journey were foreclosed. Writing for the media watch group FAIR, Alan Macleod published a piece titled, "Refugee Caravan: Lots of Coverage, Little Context," saying this:

> Indeed, there is very little discussion of why refugees are so desperate to leave their countries and travel to the US. A previous FAIR study (7/17/18) found that immigrant voices are notably absent in reporting on immigration. When any explanation is given for why people are migrating, it is extremely shallow—for example, that a gang threatened to kill them (NPR, 11/22/18) or their family (*New York Times*, (10/26/18), or that "they had a dream" to go to the US (*New York Times*, 11/30/18).[10]

Focusing on security allows media coverage to avoid a social-causal context that could explain why the migrants have left their homes. Indeed, such information would require a historical discussion of the decades of U.S. policies that have left the region permanently scarred. A security frame avoids reporting on the role played by U.S. policies, the ways in which unequal trade, multinational corporate enterprises, and internal political corruption have all led to economic decline, community impoverishment, and the cycles of violence in El Salvador, Honduras, and Guatemala.

Media frames offer an encapsulated narrative, one that begins with an "invasion" of a "marching army" of migrants, presenting them as a danger. The problem is then solved by those in power—it is up to security forces to repel them. If media began with the question of why so many people have been forced to leave their homes, news stories would have to look to conditions in those countries for answers. Turning the camera away from the issues of northern border security would point it back toward the origins of migrations from the south. These would be much different stories. Coverage would be able to identify the problems and offer far different solutions to the crisis of migration, ones that lay outside the parameters of security discourses, ones that demand information about economic inequality and environmental struggles, and a fulsome debate about U.S. policies in the region. Information about how these countries have become so poor and why migrants have become the targets of violence would spark debate about policies and the war on drug cartels, for example. Debating those issues would play a democratic role. Such a media frame would have to date back decades. It could not be told using the lexicon and logics of the current U.S. President.

We offer in this book alternative narratives able to look back on this history, ones that help explain the origins and long genesis of the current forced migrations from Central America. Looking back at U.S. policies under the Reagan Administration, we recount the U.S. role in the civil war in El Salvador and the *contra* war in Nicaragua. In Chapter 1, we look at social movements under attack as the people demanded change in El Salvador. Robin Andersen traces the media coverage that justified U.S. intervention and finds that the language and structure of security discourses distorted conditions and events taking place. The American public was misled then, and it continues to be misinformed today.

The legacy of wars in Central America continue to reverberate across the region. El Salvador is a country awash in violence, as Adrian Bergmann details in Chapter 2, "Violence, Migration, and the Perverse Effects of Gang Repression in Central America." Bergmann provides an inside view of the recent political power struggles in El Salvador, explaining the entrenched dynamic of armed violence and the causes of forced migration from the country. Offering the most recent data that calls into question the assertion that there is a crisis of migration from Central America, he argues that U.S. security policies, and those of the government of El Salvador, only serve to exacerbate the problems. He argues that security discourses and humanitarian perspectives are incompatible and have led to counterproductive policies unable to solve the problems of out migrations from the country.

In Chapters 3 and 4, we connect recent press reports of violence and deaths of migrants along the U.S. border from Honduras and Guatemala to the conditions experienced in their home countries. In 2009, the Honduran military deposed the democratically elected president, Jose Manuel Zelaya. Once again, the U.S. supported the coup that set in motion the continued destruction of democratic institutions in Honduras. Today, the current president of Honduras, Juan Orlando Hernández, is connected to the various forms of organized crime and drug traffickers that perpetrate violence against the Honduran people. As Dana Frank explains, the post-coup regime initiated the corruption of the judiciary and the police and the military. "This is a U.S. supported regime in the aftermath of a coup that led to the tremendous destruction of the rule of law in Honduras."[11] Today, the "war on drugs" justifies militarized violence in the county. It is the latest iteration of a policy that has led to brutality and destruction. In Guatemala, history follows a similar pattern, where, as historian Greg Grandin explains, indigenous peoples have been the targets of violence and repression for over a century. U.S. interventions there have been part of that process, and border patrol agencies are also implicated in the violence.

The years of militarization of the hemisphere have affected the United States as well. Nowhere is the connection between the language of demonization and violence more evident than in the United States.

Anti-Immigrant Demonization, Hate Groups, and Extremist Violence

Beginning with his campaign in 2016, candidate Trump appealed to the electorate with xenophobic language. He characterized migrants from Mexico as criminals, cultivated fears, called for greater security, and promised to build a wall between Mexico and the United States. One commentator summarized Trump's message as a generalized hostility toward all non-white, non-conventional persons, which he sees as the *Other*.[12] Such repetition, frequently featured on media, from a political leader, has been identified by the United Nations as hate speech.[13] The cultivation of hatred and the politics of fear have serious consequences. They can lead to a rise in nationalism, racism, and violence against immigrants.[14] As Heidi Beirich, Director of the Intelligence Project, Southern Poverty Law Center, noted, "There are more hate groups, more hate crimes and more domestic terrorism...It is a troubling set of circumstances."[15] As xenophobia spreads through social media,[16] global hate crimes now illustrate the consequences of such speech. On March 15, 2019, 50 people were killed, and many were injured in a hate-filled attack on two mosques in Christchurch, New Zealand. In a 74-page manifesto, the shooter identified Trump as "a symbol of renewed white identity and common purpose."[17]

In the United States, before the election in 2016, the number of hate groups had fallen for three straight years in a row. But by 2018, the Southern Poverty Law Center reports that the number of hate groups rose to over 1,000. That figure represents a 30 percent jump from 2014. The Center attributes this rise "to a toxic combination of political polarization, anti-immigrant sentiment and technologies that help spread propaganda online."[18] Heidi Beirich goes on to note that "the increase in extremist activity tracked by her team began in earnest in the early days of the 2016 presidential election."[19] Hate crimes and violence have also escalated. There has been a "30 percent increase in the number of hate crimes reported to the F.B.I. from 2015 through 2017," and the Anti-Defamation League reports a surge of right-wing violence that killed at least 50 people in 2018.[20] We argue in these pages that misinformation about immigrants and the ways they are represented, criminalized, demonized, and preyed upon, together with the politics of fear, have served to cultivate hatreds and led to the rise of hate groups, and violence against migrants, manifested in many ways.

Within the United States, the brutality and militarism of policies directed toward criminalizing the peoples of Central America are now deeply woven into the fabric of American culture, especially in the borderlands of the southwestern United States. This phenomenon is discussed in Chapter 5. Today, the U.S. border has become a militarized fortress, with migrants who arrive from Central America treated like enemies, not with the dignity and compassion demanded by long-standing humanitarian principles that understand the need for protection from violence and persecution. Instead, migrants are treated with the same brutality they experienced in their homeland. As the public watches events play out on their television screens, children die in the deserts of the southwest, and migrant mothers and their children are tear-gassed. Yet the news cycle moves on, and political discourse moves quickly back to another debate about a border wall and the latest threat to shut down the government. How has the United States, a country built by immigrants, turned away from a welcoming embrace to a fortress mentality? And how have the stories we tell ourselves about others contributed to the changing face of American culture and politics?

The current crisis should be viewed as a battle over global visions; one based in escalating violence, and another based in empathy and compassion. In the United States, the border itself has been expanded and transformed into a weaponized territory, a liminal space where all who enter become subjects of surveillance, their movements tracked and their identities as global citizens challenged or, worse, erased. As these liminal territories grow and expand, they become more dangerous. Now, by the time migrants reach the U.S. border, they are on the verge of collapse, weakened, and injured by an American landscape turned into a battlefield. As *The Guardian* newspaper reported, the death of a seven-year-old Guatemalan girl named Jakelin is further evidence of how "the harsh desert terrain along the southwestern border is used 'as a weapon' to deter migrants, according to a humanitarian non-profit, No More Deaths."[21] The Non-governmental Organization's (NGO's) 2016 report into border security polices found that U.S. authorities are utilizing "the landscape as a weapon to slow down, injure, and apprehend [migrants]." As large swaths of borderlands are weaponized, aid workers are charged with crimes for trying to prevent more migrants from dying. On January 20, 2019, four volunteers were convicted of leaving water and food in the desert, and are currently facing sentences of six months in prison. As one of the women asked, "If giving water to someone dying of thirst is illegal, what humanity is left in the law of this country?"[22]

These laws, policies, and perspectives are greatly influenced by a world viewed through the lens of security discourses. The current escalation of the militarization of the United States and its borders are part of a long history of U.S. policies toward the people of Central America. As a critique of those policies, and an argument for an alternative vision, this book hopes to make an intervention into the dynamics of militarism and the weaponizing of global territories, and help break the long-standing and persistent cycles of violence that continue to destroy the homes and peoples of the Americas.

Notes

1 Chris Pleasance, "Pro-migration Firebrand who Started the Migrant Caravan: Honduran Radio Host Encouraged People to Band Together for Safety... Now There are 14,000 of Them," *Daily Mail,* October 24, 2018, www.dailymail.co.uk/news/article-6310583/Honduran-radio-host-revealed-man-migrant-caravan.html

2 Mehdi Hasan, "From Caravans to Cages: Why Trump Bases Immigrants," *Deconstructed Podcast, The Intercept*, October 25, 2018,

https://theintercept.com/2018/10/25/from-caravans-to-cages-why-trump-bashes-migrants/

3 Robert Parry and Peter Kornbluh, "Iran-Contra's Untold Story," *Foreign Policy* 72, Fall (1988): 3–30.

4 Brandon Darby, "Leaked Images Reveal Children Warehoused in Crowded U.S. Cells, Border Patrol Overwhelmed," Breitbart, June 5, 2014, www.breitbart.com/texas/2014/06/05/leaked-images-reveal-children-warehoused-in-crowded-us-cells-border-patrol-overwhelmed/

5 Kristin Tate, "Go to America with Your Child, You Won't Get Turned Away," Breitbart, June 5, 2014, www.breitbart.com/texas/2014/06/05/go-to-america-with-your-child-you-wont-get-turned-away/

6 Robert Entman, "Framing: Towards Clarification of a Fractured Paradigm," *Journal of Communication* 43, no. 4: 51–8 (1993), www.academia.edu/13166309/Framing_Towards_Clarification_of_a_Fractured_Paradigm

7 William A. Gamson and M.A. Wolfsfeld, "Movements and Media as Interacting Systems," *Annals of the American Academy of Political and Social Science* 528 (1993): 4–125.

8 Sei-Hill Kim, John Carvalho, Andrew Davis, and Amanda Mullins, "The View of the Border: News Framing of the Definition, Causes, and Solutions to Illegal Immigration," *Mass Communication and Society* 4, no. 3 (2011): 292–314, https://psycnet.apa.org/record/2011-10398-002

9 Mary Ann Glendon, *A World Made New: Eleanor Roosevelt and the Universal Declaration of Human Rights* (New York: Random House, 2001).

10 Alan Macleod, "Refugee Caravan: Lots of Coverage Little Context," FAIR, December 13, 2018, https://fair.org/home/refugee-caravan-lots-of-coverage-little-context/

11 *Democracy Now*, "It's not a Natural Disaster: Dana Frank on How US-Back Coup in Honduras Fueled Migrant Crisis," October 28, 2018, www.democracynow.org/2018/11/28/it_is_not_a_natural_disaster

12 Jim Conn, "In Search of a National Dialogue on Race," *Salon.com*, September 27, 2016, www.alternet.org/culture/search-national-dialogue-race?akid=14690.19806.G4PgoV&rd=1&src=newsletter1064390&t=14

13 Adama Dieng and Simona Cruciani, "When Media is Used to Incite Violence: The United Nations, Genocide and Atrocity Crimes," in *Routledge Companion to Media and Humanitarian Action*, ed. Robin Andersen and Purnaka de Silva (New York; Routledge, 2018).

14 United Nations, General Assembly, "Third Committee Experts Warn Racism, Hate Speech, White Supremacy to Become Mainstream Unless States Enforce Zero-Tolerance Policies, Prevent Exclusion," Seventy-third Session, 37th & 38th Meetings, October 29, 2918. www.un.org/press/en/2018/gashc4245.doc.htm

15 Liam Stack, "Over 1,000 Hate Groups are Active in the United States, Civil Rights Group Says," *New York Times*, February 20, 2019, www.nytimes.com/2019/02/20/us/hate-groups-rise.html

16 Robin Andersen, "Weaponizing Social Media: The 'Alt-Right,' the Election of Donald Trump and the Rise of Ethno-Nationalism in the United States," in *Routledge Companion to Media and Humanitarian Action*, ed. Robin Andersen and Purnaka de Silva (New York; Routledge, 2018).

17 Al Jazeera, "New Zealand Mosque Attacks Suspect Praised Trump in Manifesto," March 16, 2019, https://www.aljazeera.com/news/2019/03/zealand-mosques-attack-suspect-praised-trump-manifesto-190315100143150.html

18 Ibid., Liam Stack 2019.

19 Ibid., Liam Stack 2019.

20 Ibid., Liam Stack 2019.

21 Lauren Aratani, "Death of Guatemalan Migrant Girl Highlights Hardline Border Policy," *The Guardian*, December 15, 2018, www.theguardian.com/us-news/2018/dec/15/mexico-border-terrain-weapon-us-migrants

22 Rafael Carranza, "Four Aid Volunteers Found Guilty of Dropping Off Water, Food for Migrants in Arizona," *USA Today*, January 20, 2019, www.usatoday.com/story/news/nation/2019/01/20/volunteers-guilty-dropping-water-food-migrants-arizona-desert/2632435002/

1 From the Civil War in El Salvador to MS-13

Media Frames that Distort, Mislead, and Omit

Robin Andersen

President Trump's First State of the Union Address

In his first State of the Union address on January 30, 2018, Donald Trump claimed that illegal immigrants "have caused the loss of many innocent lives." Paying special attention to the transnational gang known as MS-13 (also called Mara Salvatrucha or "gang of Salvadoran guys"), the President said that many of its members "took advantage of glaring loopholes in our laws to enter the country as unaccompanied alien minors" and then ended up murdering American citizens.[1] He cited the brutal deaths of two Long Island teenagers Kayla Cuevas and Nisa Mickens, killed by the gang in 2016. Television cameras focused on the parents strategically seated in the audience as they cried listening to the story of their children's murders. Trump then proposed increasing border security to no longer allow gang members "to break into our country."[2]

Evelyn Rodriguez, the mother of Kayla Cuevas, had become an advocate for gang prevention efforts in schools, but she had declined to campaign against illegal immigration.[3] Before boarding the plane to Washington to attend the address, Rodriguez told the *New York Times*, "I want him [Trump] to ensure that we're going to get the proper funding for the resources for our kids." She added, "I'm not here for anybody's political gain."[4] Trump nevertheless featured her as a prime victim of immigrant crime, not as someone pressing for school funding and crime prevention. In this way, images of bereaved family members were cynically used as strategic persuasion for Trump's version of the immigration narrative. The President's claim that MS-13 entered the United States illegally is false. The characterization that they "broke into our country," is also false. The gang was formed by young Salvadoran refugee on the streets of Los Angeles who came to the United States in the 1980s after fleeing the U.S.-backed civil war. In effect, the United States had broken into their country.

Academic researchers and journalists who study the origins and growth of MS-13 offer a very different narrative than that of the President. Writing in the *Washington Post* the day after the speech, Jose Miguel Cruz of Florida International University, pointed out that the gang did not come from south of the border.[5] In fact it was "founded in Los Angeles in the 1980s by children of Salvadoran immigrants who fled a brutal civil war, a war which was substantially funded by the United States." The early members were displaced teenagers who hung out on street corners in Southern California's underprivileged communities. By the mid-1980s, as urban neighborhoods became the focus of new racialized street-level law enforcement tactics of the war on drugs, immigrant communities were targeted by police sweeps. Many young men were arrested in massive "anti-gang" operations in Los Angeles and incarcerated. Then in 1996, The Clinton administration enacted the Illegal Immigration Reform and Immigrant Responsibility Act, deporting thousands of foreign-born residents convicted of crimes. Gang members went from California jails to Central American streets.[6] As Cruz notes, the consequences of the deportations of young men who were now criminalized, and strangers in the countries where they were born, were dire. Gang members were turned loose on El Salvador and its neighbors, Honduras, and Mexico. In its SOTU coverage, the *New York Times* also mentioned the gang's origins, though in an abbreviated form saying, "MS-13 was formed in Los Angeles in the 1980s by refugees from El Salvador escaping civil war." Robbins added, "In the mid-1990s, the government started deporting the immigrant gang members, which helped grow its leadership base in El Salvador."[7] She does not mention that the United States backed the civil war. Reporting on the SOTU, CBS coverage augmented the President's words by giving details and adding material about the brutality of MS-13,

> In 2012, MS-13 was designated a transnational criminal organization by the Treasury Department, which said the gang is involved in "serious transnational criminal activities, including drug trafficking, kidnapping, human smuggling, sex trafficking, murder, assassinations, racketeering, blackmail, extortion, and immigration offenses."

No mention is made of the gang's U.S. origin, or the civil war in El Salvador.

Democracy Now and the *Washington Post* were two of the few news outlets that provided background on MS-13. Both featured academics who detailed some of the complex history that created the gang. By contrast, most mainstream media debate was restricted to a narrow set of terms about how to characterize immigration policy, and statistics demonstrating that not all migrants are criminals. In response to President Trump's SOTU speech, many mainstream news outlets featured politicians who challenged Trump's statements. *USA Today* repeated Kamala Harris's interview with Chris Matthews after the speech in which "she slammed" the president saying, "to equate that with DREAMers and DACA was completely irresponsible, and it was scapegoating and it was fear-mongering and it was wrong." Though these words amount to meaningful criticism, they are only a glimpse of a humanitarian perspectives, and they do not connect with the broader picture of migration, or the causes of forced migrations from Central America.

Whereas mainstream, commercial media failed to provide adequate response to Trump's first SOTU speech, over the course of 2018, Hannah Dreier, a young reporter working for the non-profit news outlet *ProPublica*, wrote a series of articles about MS-13 activities on Long Island. The series, *Trapped in Gangland*, revealed that anti-immigrant rhetoric and police bias were undermining efforts to combat the gang as it continued to prey on Latino teenagers. In "The Disappeared,"[8] Dreier follows a mother searching for her missing son in a nearby woods called the "killing fields." The story exposed the indifference of the Suffolk County Police when confronted with nearly a dozen Latino teenagers who went missing in 2016 and 2017. Overall, the stories examined the impact of the gang and law enforcement on the region's growing Latino community, and amplified the experiences of those who are seldom heard from in the debate about border security and MS-13."[9] In 2019, *ProPublica*, who partnered with *New York* magazine, *Newsday*, and the *New York Times Magazine* to publish the articles, won its fifth Pulitzer Prize for the series.

Without these perspectives, the immigration debate is inevitably shallow and easily distorted.

Professional standards of journalism define news primarily as timely, events oriented reporting. Historical frames, especially those that contradict conventional narratives are largely absent from public discourse. Television images serve to augment and engage the shallow narratives that often substitute for coherence and background. At the SOTU address, bereaved relatives added visual "evidence" for false narratives proposed by a president willing to mislead the public on immigration and offer false solutions to the murders of American teenagers.

To illuminate the causes and origins of the forced migrations of Central American refugees, and the long origins of the violence now experienced there, we will now turn to the role U.S. foreign policy played for decades in destabilizing the region.

The History of U.S. Militarism in Central America

Only five years after the Vietnam War finally came to an end in 1975, the United States would fight a series of counterinsurgency wars, this time in Central America. These would be proxy wars, funded by the United States but fought by Central Americans trained by U.S. advisors. Helicopter gunships carried brown-skinned soldiers pointing automatic weapons down on rebel-held territory in the northern mountains of El Salvador. They would become the visual icons of war in Central America.[10] With the help of U.S. advisors and the Central Intelligence Agency, on the ground along the mountain ridges that separate Honduras from Nicaragua, a *contra* army would be assembled.[11] Comprised mainly of former security forces who had been in the employ of deposed Nicaraguan dictator, Anastasio Somoza, they would slip across the Honduran border into Nicaragua. Their violent raids targeted civilians, and are now widely understood to the tactics of non-state terrorism.[12] These raids persisted even though it was widely understood that *contras* routinely engaged in human rights violations.[13] The Reagan Administration insisted that the attacks were necessary to overthrow the revolutionary Sandinista government.

The Reagan Administration produced a White Paper claiming that the Soviet Union was "meddling" in "our" hemisphere.[14] Unless the United States intervened militarily it argued, the countries of Central America would fall like dominoes to the communist onslaught.[15] According to the White Paper, the Soviets were funneling guns through Nicaragua to the rebels fighting against the U.S.-supported government in El Salvador. By 1981, Ronald Reagan began the "low-intensity warfare," in a neo-cold war policy that proclaimed the *contras* were "freedom fighters," the equivalent of our founding fathers. Contras, Reagan asserted, were America's only hope against Soviet communism, which had turned Nicaragua into a "totalitarian dungeon."[16] The contras were skillfully packaged using a variety of media technique aimed at shaping U.S.

public opinion in favor of what was actually a rag-tag army illegally funded by the White House.[17] None of the "evidence" offered by the C.I.A. or other U.S. intelligence agencies that the Soviets were attempting to destabilize Central America was ever verified.[18]

In the face of opposition from Congress and the American people, officials in the Reagan White House would resort to illegal means to finance the proxy war, and the summer of 1987, America viewers would be transfixed by live coverage of Congressional hearings investigating executive branch wrong-doing in the Iran Contra scandal.[19] Because of years of effective press management in framing the Central American neo-cold war by the executive branch, the press completely missed the story. As *Washington Post* editors Leonard Downie and Robert Kaiser admitted in 2002, "We didn't get one of the biggest stories of the decade until it was handed to us on a platter."[20]

We can ask certain questions about the Central America wars of the 1980s, such as: How was information about these conflicts framed, and what kinds of official interpretations were constructed to legitimate these policies? What did Americans know of these actions and did they support them? With documentation of human rights abuses, and terrible atrocities committed by the para-military and security forces, how did American institutions, including the press, and the American public respond to the loss of life of so many innocent people? The answers to these questions will help illuminate the conflict and the consequences of U.S. involvement in Central America, and lead us to new understandings about why the history of U.S. militarism in the region is so rarely invoked in media discourse about twenty-first century Central American refugees.

An appropriate place to begin recounting this history is the coup in El Salvador in 1979. The interruption it caused intermingled with another set of confounding images shown on TV from a different part of the world, the shocking pictures of Americans held hostage in Iran. As the decade pressed on Central America and Iran would be surprisingly paired as unlikely cohorts united by their geopolitical importance to the neo-cold warriors of the twentieth century, who it would be reveled, sold weapons to the regime responsible for kidnapping Americans and used the money to arm the *contras*. Today, the regions of the Middle East and Central America remain mired in conflict and comprise the source countries for most of the forced migrations of refugee under attack by the current Trump Administration's policies.

The Coup in El Salvador

On October 15, 1979, a Revolutionary Government Junta (JRG) deposed then President General Carlos Humberto Romero in a civil-military coup in El Salvador. The coup reportedly brought to power a moderate government composed of civilian and military officials willing to make structural changes within Salvadoran society. This premise formed the foundation of media coverage and conferred legitimacy on the Salvadoran Army. The narrative followed these parameters. Brutality in the person of General Romero had been overthrown, and a just society was in the making. Official statements from the U.S. government and the new ruling junta went like this. Young progressive military officers had ousted Romero, a right-wing general and the perpetrator of brutal repression, who had ruled the country with an iron fist. The corrupt system of social and economic injustice maintained through force by police and military would stop. Rightwing oligarchs, who up to that point had kept the wealth of the country to themselves, were to relinquish a small fraction of their privilege and a fledgling, lawful democracy would replace revolution. The "left" would be appeased with reforms, and "extremists" would be controlled. Most importantly, the status quo would be preserved and U.S. interests would be safe.[21]

The sources of injustice was aptly described in this scenario. The country had been dominated by a wealthy, powerful elite for decades, a structure that led to poverty and injustice, maintained only through military repression. That admission was true, but the system was not about to change. The junta never lived up to the characterization of "moderate," even though news coverage consistently made that claim.

It was true that reform-minded officers were among those who led the coup. They did promise to begin the process that would abolish injustice, and they asked civilians to join them in the task of restructuring Salvadoran society. In *El Salvador: The Face of Revolution*, authors Robert Armstrong and Janet Shenk characterized these civilians as "men of impeccable democratic credentials."[22] In the beginning, the junta was a coalition of military and civilian progressives willing to work for change. It also included right-wing conservatives such as Jose Guillermo Garcia and Jaime Abdule Gutierrez who led the hard-line faction of the military. Leaders representing a more progressive military, together with civilian officials would struggle to gain control over security forces for the three months following the coup, a battle they would lose against the power of the right-wing Generals.

Media Coverage

The 1979 coup in El Salvador caught the attention of the media, especially television, which, as reporter Mort Rosenblum observed in *Coups and Earthquakes,* values stories about disruption and chaos in the developing world.[23] The sense the press made of the story of the coup was the result of a particular combination of television's distain for historical context, its fascination with conflict and drama, and its willingness to, if not believe, then repeat official statements and versions of events. Such stories were usually hastily constructed during conversations at the Intercontinental Hotel in San Salvador, which often took place after embassy briefings.

The "Moderate" Junta that Never Was

From the beginning, television news reports characterized the junta as centrist and moderate:

> The State Department in Washington said the leadership appeared centrist and moderate...
>
> NBC, October 16, 1979

> The State Department said today the new military government in El Salvador appears to be moderate and its first statements are encouraging...
>
> ABC, October 16, 1979

On October 18, 1979, CBS reported the appointment of civilians to the new government:

> Three civilians considered sympathizers of the moderate opposition party were appointed to serve on the junta...

This CBS report goes on to describe the "moderate" credentials of Roman Mayorga, a former university president, and a man educated at MIT. This would be the last report on the structure and nature of the junta. From this time on it is labeled "reform-minded," "moderate," "centrist," or "civilian/military." Although the moderate label solidified, the centrist junta did not materialize. Almost immediately the progressive officers and civilians found it impossible to control the actions of the right-wing elements within the military. As one human rights report confirmed, military abuses continued. Civilians in the junta soon found their

influence over the army was limited or in the case of the
National Guard and the Treasury Police, virtually non-existent.
Members of the latter two branches of the Security Forces
also belonged to various paramilitary groups that played an
ever-more-violent role in the last months of 1979.[24]

On December 29, 1979, Salvador Samayoa, then Minister of Education, and Enrique Alvarez Cordova, Minister of Agriculture, along
with three other civilian members from the first junta resigned
in protest. After three months of internal struggles they realized
they could not control the army and stop the brutality. Then on
January 3, 1980, Guillermo Ungo and Roman Mayorga resigned
along with virtually the entire cabinet and all high-ranking officials. In the words of Armstrong and Shenk "The center had col-
lapsed."[25] This interpretation corroborated the human rights
report that stated, "With the fall of the "First Junta" the centrist
alternative was effectively closed, and the conservatives were back
in unquestioned control."[26]

None of the networks reported any of these events, nor the final
resignation of the junta members. For television news viewers, these
political developments never happened, yet the government continued to be labeled moderate. A report aired on NBC never mentioned
that any of these struggles were taking place: "The leftists oppose
the moderate junta which took power here last October." Even after
the resignations as late as February 19, 1980, NBC reported, "The
Carter Administration is considering proposals to send military
advisors to help bolster the moderate government now in power."
The government was labeled moderate even when it seemed to be a
contradiction in terms: "The ruling moderate junta clamped a news
blackout on radio stations" (CBS January 23, 1980).

Though the final blow to the centrist position came at the beginning of 1980, it must be remembered that the junta was never
in control of the security forces. The army never acted in a moderate way. The civilians finally resigned because they realized
that they were the democratic face that shielded the military from
criticism. In spite of continuing demands for reform, and contrary
to what TV news reported, repression actually increased after the
coup. Security Forces acted with the same brutality as those under
Romero, and within a week, the government was held responsible
for more than 100 killings of demonstrators and striking workers.[27]

Independent sources described continued and escalating military abuses against major sectors of the population. But this might

not have been so surprising to viewers had they known the long history of political inequality, army repression, and economic disparities in El Salvador.

The Historical Void

Explaining even a little of the uncontested history of El Salvador at the time would have provided a context for understanding the internal power struggles tearing the new government apart. The legacy of colonialism had left most Central American countries controlled by economic elites, but nowhere, with the possible exception of Guatemala, was their power as complete and long reigning as in El Salvador. The Salvadoran oligarchy, the small group of families who controlled the country's wealth, survived and grew richer because of their willingness to make alliances with the armed forces. Decades of social and economic injustice were maintained by security forces and their more unofficial paramilitary death squads. While the wealthy made money, the colonels and generals kept the poor, the workers, and the peasants under control, too terrified to rebel. Democratic elections over the years had been stolen, when progressives had been voted in they were either killed or forced to flee. The political arena had been effectively closed as a mechanism for reform. Amid this background, the coup took place.

That moderate civilians within the junta were not able to end the years of military repression most clearly evidenced by the continued military and para-military attacks on demonstrations. The rights to peaceful assembly and to organize unions, which had been declared illegal in the past, were to have been ushered in with the new junta. But instead of fulfilling its promise of reform, continuing attacks were documented by the Americas Watch Committee and the American Civil Liberties Union which states: "Although the Proclamation issued following the coup guaranteed the establishment of (political) parties of all ideologies" and recognized "the right to unionize, in all labor sectors," attacks on unionists continued to take place almost from the outset.[28]

Shortly after the coup, television news condoned government brutality against peaceful demonstrators with these words:

> El Salvador's new government today made its first get tough reply to protesting leftists since the coup there two weeks ago...

Troops fired into a crowd of about 200 demonstrators in the capital, they wounded twenty two.

CBS, October 30, 1979

Demonstrations were a frequent topic for news stories during this period, and resulted in some of the most distorted and misleading news coverage. As demonstrators became the victims of army attacks, the resulting images of chaos had entertainment value. An exciting story of disruption could be told, complete with people running from sniper fire, jerky "documentary" camera style, corpses in the streets, and the screams of Red Cross ambulance sirens—and of the wounded.

The Precursor to Today's Security Discourses: The Law and Order Frame

With very little background on the region journalists relied on a standard media framework, one that could accommodate such dramatic visual footage. They would focus on chaos as the theme and feature those who promised to restore law and order. British theorists identified such conventional treatment by the BBC in reporting crime and urban riots, and described the framework as "dangerously pre-emptive and frequently mythical."[29] Not surprisingly, the most important structural element of the law and order frame is violence.

In the Central American country of El Salvador the leftist fight against the new military junta there intensified...

ABC, November 4, 1979

The conflict in El Salvador is portrayed as having been initiated by leftists, and/or demonstrators. Other stories use labels, such as guerrillas, extremists, students, or some variation thereof. The leftists are always attacking, fighting, or rebelling against the newly established government. The impression is that the legitimate "moderate" government is under siege by attackers who threaten the fundamental social order.

Dramatic conflict, especially visually depicted, is exciting, and gains the attention of the viewer and as the crisis unfolds viewers watch to see how the violence will end. Opening footage of the narrative structure presents a situation of chaos and the disruption that poses a problem for *those in power*. It calls upon authorities to react, demanding that order be restored. In the news stories of El Salvador, the agents of law and order are the army and the security forces directed by the new junta. It is they who react to "leftist" violence, and after a battle, restore order. The "leftists," cause the problem and are set in dramatic conflict with legitimate force:

> El Salvador's new government today made its first get-tough *reply* to protesting leftists... [emphasis added]
>
> CBS, October 28, 1979

Strengthening of the agents of law and order is always presented as defensive, reactive, and necessary. They "had to be" called in, and they had to "get tough." In acting out this drama between leftists and security forces, the scales are always tilted in favor of those in positions of state-sanctioned power. When the law and order frame is used to cover a country such as El Salvador where the status quo is maintained by force, the leftist demonstrator/rioter is not only within the realm of the arrestable, but within that of the killable, as this CBS story shows: "But so far leftist uprisings have failed, seventeen people were killed in San Marcos when the army quashed a guerrilla takeover of that city" (CBS, October 18, 1979). The information that 17 people were killed is portrayed as a necessary consequence of the army's obligation to restore order. The added use of the word "quashed" makes it also seem somehow gentle, as if brute force were not really exerted. Within the law and order context, putting down uprisings is a positive act. The consequence of the frame, then, is to make the killing of leftists, and even "innocent" people, a palatable event; a necessary, if lamentable, outcome of restoring order to chaos.

Video news from little-know counties that emphasize action drama contain almost no context, and the little information offered distorts the viewers understanding of events. The narrative introduced a crisis, pitted characters against one another, was filled in with shots fired, and ends with a body count. The drama of leftists battling with security forces was fast-paced and exciting, and therefore entertaining. Closure was effected when calm returned and the forces of order were once again in control, if only temporarily. Such contained, rushed stories never seem to pause to ask why demonstrations and attacks are happening. These actions appear to be totally without history, motivation, or political purpose. They come flashing out of a mysterious void—as if from nowhere.[30] In place of explanation comes the familiar assertion that those who cause violence, usually leftist, are simply extremists by nature. "Notions of causality are tautological in the mythic sense—a criminal is criminal is criminal."[31] For other explanations to come into play, the site of the problem would need to shift from the focus on violence to the world of *conditions that precipitated* such startling conflict.

A brief look at the last event before the onset of civil war underscores the ways in which violence and attacks are foregrounded at the expense of social reasoning and causal explanations.

The Mass March: Peaceful Protest Attacked

On January 22, 1980, largest mass demonstration in the history of the country took place in San Salvador. It represented a broad coalition of popular organizations and a country whose majority population was unified against a repressive government.

Armstrong and Shenk write:

> Thousands and yet again thousands of shabbily dressed Salvadorans surged toward the crossroads and... took their places behind the standard bearers of the different popular organizations. At 1:00 a.m., the demonstration stretched...twenty blocks from the crossroads and out to the nearest hill slopes on either side of the Avenida Guerrero. There were columns of state employees, organized slum dwellers, factory workers, electricians, teachers and, endlessly, the farmworkers and peasants who had slipped through the roadblocks to enter the capital before dawn.[32]

It is impossible for the television viewer to understand the significance of a mass opposition movement of this magnitude in a thirty-second television news report that focuses on the few seconds of gunfire. Hours of massive protest characterized by orderliness, discipline, and diversity were reduced to these words:

> An anti-government march through San Salvador today by 50,000 leftists turned into a shooting match with unidentified snipers on rooftops. At least twenty persons were reported killed and twenty-seven wounded.
>
> CBS, January 22, 1980

Armstrong and Shenk blame the attack on the military, not "unidentified" gunmen. As the march moved toward the downtown square shots rang out, "the thudding booms characteristic of the military's regulation G-3 machine gun, a combat weapon thoroughly inappropriate for routine urban police needs, yet carried by all security forces as well as the army."[33] The army was not creating order, but chaos out of what would otherwise have been a peaceful demonstration. Armstrong and Shenk conclude their account of the day, at the point in which the television drama would begin: "The first bodies slumped to the ground in front of the cathedral, and as the now terrified crowd broke ranks and scattered down the side streets and into nearby buildings."

If the focal point of news coverage were shifted from violence to problems of political, social, economic, and repressive realities, an entirely different set of solutions and outcomes responding to questions of social causality would necessarily come into play. Issues would emerge such as whether attempts were being made to resolve existing social inequities within the country, such as improvements in working and living conditions. Resolutions would consist of, for example, agreeing to fair wages and safe working conditions, allowing for better housing and nutrition, providing public services, such as drinkable water, electric power, and sanitation, just to list a few. It would mean, in essence, pointing out the necessity for economic reform, which was the alleged objective for the October 15th coup. Above all, it would mean solving the problem of military abuses. Security forces would fall well within the realm of problems, instead of being looked to for solutions.

The Beginning of the Civil War: Archbishop Romero and the Church Women

The country began its decent into a full-blown civil war as the period of open political struggle came to an end. Unable to protect themselves against paramilitary violence and from army fire in the face of legal, peaceful, actions, and unable to achieve social and economic justice in the political arena, many people left San Salvador and retreated to rural areas. Violence by the military and paramilitary security forces escalated but it was harder to document in the countryside than it had been in the more open urban context of San Salvador. The rebels took up arms and formed the FMLN, the Farabundo Marti National Liberation Front. The Carter Administration sent more military aid to the Army, now led by the hard-right wing General Garcia, and failed to enter into diplomatic negotiations that could have resulted in real reform, and a negotiated peace. Intensive diplomatic pressure from the United States might well have ended the war before it gained momentum.

By the end of 1980, the brutality of the security forces was already well documented, yet the United States continued to fund the Salvadoran military. The war would personally confront then U.S. Ambassador Robert White, when he peered down into the graves of four American churchwomen in December. Catholics who worked in poor and underserved neighborhoods were not exempt from right-wing death squads. The nuns had been kidnapped on the way back from the airport returning to the poor communities they served. Raped and murdered, their bodies were thrown in hastily dug graves along the road they traveled.

They were not the first to die in the religious community. Like the church women, the much beloved and respected Archbishop Óscar Arnulfo Romero was a voice for the poor and repressed. An outspoken critic of right-wing violence, from the pulpit of his church in San Salvador he openly criticized the military for brutality and asked them to lay down their guns.

> There is an institutionalized violence that provokes the anger of the people. It is a violence that comes from the right. They want to maintain their privileges through oppressive means. The oppressed, on the other hand, react to this violence and are labeled leftist. But as long as the violence from the right continues, then the right is to blame for this situation.[34]

Archbishop Romero was assassinated in March 1980. A week after his death Romero's funeral was held in the plaza outside the main cathedral in San Salvador. As thousands of mourners crowded into the square, army snipers and para-military gunmen stationed on rooftops opened fire. That day 42 people were killed and more than 200 were wounded. The event marked the beginning of El Salvador's 12-year civil war, in which tens of thousands of people died before a peace accord was signed in January of 1992.[35]

Investigations of the army to find those responsible for the murders of the churchwomen were begun, but another U.S. President was elected in November of 1980. Ronald Reagan would pursue the military option in earnest, Jimmy Carter having let slip the moment when war could have been prevented.

"Extremists on Both the Left and the Right"

The mystification of violence was continued and reached levels of absurdity by the end of the Carter years. The incredible loss of human life at the hands of the death-squads and security forces was always "caused by extremists on both the left and the right." The moderate label affixed to the government defined as the "center" held tight through numerous reshufflings, even in the face of executions and murders tied to the armed forces. Because television is a system of internal references, the constellation of law and order has itself become, for the U.S. media, the history of El Salvador. In this way, a national movement born out of military repression and social injustice could be explained by the new President, Ronald Reagan as an external contest between two superpowers, Democracy against the Evil Empire.

The Reagan Years and The White Paper

Ronald Reagan came to power in 1980 and within a matter of months began to sell the public on a new justification for conflict—the neo-cold war.

In March of 1981, the new Reagan White House released a "White Paper," a document that would come to define the Reagan Doctrine and its strategy to reinvigorate a pre-Vietnam Cold War atmosphere. The policy paper "drew the line" against communism in the hemisphere. In Nicaragua, the Sandinistas had successfully taken power from the U.S.-backed Somoza dictatorship, and The White Paper claimed to include evidence that the Sandinistas were arming the rebels in El Salvador. It was "the funnel" through which communism was being spread into our hemisphere. The Reagan Doctrine called for escalating military support to the Salvadoran military, now headed by the hard-line General, Jose Guillermo Garcia. The architects of the Reagan Doctrine would assert that negotiations with the Sandinistas and the rebels in El Salvador were impossible, and only military solutions could be advanced. Thus was the Cold War reborn as Reagan popularized his favorite borrowed phrase for the Soviet Union, the Evil Empire.

Television news reported the allegations contained in the White Paper almost verbatim, one ABC anchorman held before the cameras what he called a "phone-book" size report containing "evidence" of communist interference in Central America. Only later would it be acknowledged that the White Paper contained no evidence for such claims. Not one shipment of arms from Nicaragua into El Salvador was ever found.[36]

Press coverage of the region increased by an order of magnitude as it became the geopolitical focus of Ronald Reagan's foreign policy. The agenda for what would be considered newsworthy emanated from Washington, and the policy debate about El Salvador shifted from an internal focus, to external communist meddling in "our" hemisphere. The axis of discussion was now framed around a simple choice between supporting the Salvadoran military and U.S. national security interests, or letting the country fall to communists. U.S. embassy personnel were replaced and almost overnight this new language of national security dominated policy discussions and became the media lens through which El Salvador was viewed.[37] Security discourses had firmly taken hold in the media.

Challenges from a Human Rights Perspective

Yet human rights remained the stumbling block for Reagan's new policies. So many people had already been killed, and human rights had been on the press agenda while Carter was in office and the accelerating abuses kept it there. The foreign press corps was well aware that the dead bodies carelessly thrown along the roadsides most mornings, and left in front of their own hotels[38] were the work of the paramilitary death squads. Reagan replaced Carter's U.S. Ambassador, Robert White with Dean Hinton, but the deaths of the nuns and the lay worker had affected White in a profound way. Human rights organizations, church leaders, policy critics, and solidarity groups all lined up against these new policies that they understood would lead to increased brutality against civilians. This combined with considerable opposition from lawmakers led congress to pass an amendment to the Foreign Assistance Act of 1961. The language required the president to certify that the Salvadoran government was "making a concerted and significant effort to comply with internationally recognized human rights." Congress wanted to see the military and "elements in its own armed forces" brought under control "so as to bring to an end the indiscriminate torture and murder of Salvadoran citizens by these forces." Certification would be required periodically as a condition of continued funding for the Salvadoran military. The continuous certification process would have the effect of keeping critical comments about Central American policy, mostly by congressional Democrats, an aspect of mainstream media coverage. But by the end of Reagan's first year in office, the humanitarian costs of this new cold war would prove to be greater than almost anyone had imagined.

The El Mozote Massacre

On December 15, 1981, Reverend William Wipfler, director of the human-rights office of the National Council of Churches in New York, wrote a telegram to Ambassador Dean Hinton at the Embassy in San Salvador asking him "for confirmation or otherwise" about "reliable reports" that indicate "that between December 10 and 13 joint military and security forces operation took place in Morazan Department which resulted in over 900 civilian deaths." Reverend Wipfler had received a call from Roberto Cuellar at Socorro Juridico, the human-rights organization of the Archbishopric of San Salvador, who heard from members and friends of the church who lived in the zone that the American trained and outfitted Atlacatl Brigade had carried out a massacre at El Mozote and in the neighboring village of La Joya. Survivors of the Army's "limpieza" of the rural hamlets, roughly translated as "cleaning," had notified Cuellar and he told Wipfler that eyewitnesses had been to the site and evidence of the killings remained intact.

Getting the Story

By January 3, photojournalist Susan Meiselas and the *New York Times* correspondent Raymond Bonner were peering through the darkness trying to follow their guide down a rocky trail in the mountains of Morazan. They reached the bank of a small river and in the moonlight, they took off their clothes, put them in their backpacks and held them above their heads to cross the cold rushing water and follow the trail beyond that led to El Mozote. Ray Bonner would later admit, "I was scared shitless."[39]

Bonner travelled with photojournalist Susan Meiselas whose documentation of the region's conflict was already extensive. Bonner and Meiselas hiked all night through the mountains and reached the rebel's camp at dawn where scattered tents among the trees housed about 30 people. At daybreak on January 6th, three days after leaving the Honduran border area on foot, the two American's walked into what had been the town of El Mozote, almost a month after the massacre. There they saw bodies and parts of bodies, destroyed houses, and total destruction. Meiselas remembers a group of 14 bodies in a cornfield on the outskirts of the village, and she could "see on their faces the horrors of what had happened to them."[40]

The two were met by free-lancer Alma Guillermoprieto who was writing for the *Washington Post*. She recounts the journey as arduous. Guillermoprieto would later recall the traumatizing sensation as she walked through the nearby town of Arambala, with its pretty, white washed adobe houses, where "whole families had been blown away—these recognizable human beings, in their little dresses, just lying there mummifying in the sun."[41] Forty-five minutes away she started to smell El Mozote. As she wrote in the *Washington Post*, "The overwhelming initial impression was of the sickly sweet smell of decomposing bodies."[42]

On January 27, 1982, the *New York Times* published Ray Bonner's report describing what he found in El Mozote and the surrounding area, and Alma Guillermoprieto's story appeared the same day in the *Washington Post*. Both papers carried the stories on the front page. Bonner's story begins, "From interviews with people who live in this small mountain village and surrounding hamlets, it is clear that a massacre of major proportions occurred here last month." He describes "the charred skulls and bones of dozens of bodies buried under burned out roofs, beams and shattered tiles." He interviewed the survivor, 38-year-old Rufina Amaya, whose husband was killed along with, "her 9-year-old son and three daughters, ages 5 years, 3 years, and 8 months." (For years, Rufina would continue to tell her eyewitness account but only after the war ended and the site was exhumed, would her story be considered credible.) Bonner's story continues, "Many of the peasants were shot in their homes, but the soldiers dragged others from their houses and the church and put them in lines, women in one and men in another." During this confusion Rufina had managed to escape. In El Mozote, Guillermoprieto was shown the ruin of the little church in the central square. "The smaller sacristy beside it also appeared to have had its adobe walls pushed in. Inside, the stench was overpowering, and countless bits of bones—sculls, rib cages, femurs, a spinal column—poked out of the rubble."

These stories represent independent investigative reporting at its best, and one of the most courageous examples of newsgathering in a war zone documenting one of the worse cases of twentieth century war crimes in the new world. They included corroborating victim testimony, a stunning eyewitness account of what had happened from a survivor, on-site descriptive reporting from an undisturbed scene of mass murder by three correspondents working for different organizations, and two rolls of film shoot by an experienced photojournalist. Yet these stories were discredited, the massacre denied, and the sources attacked. The story of El Mozote would linger in a twilight of uncertainty for more than a decade.

The day after the stories appeared in the mainstream press, President Ronald Reagan signed and sent to Congress the certification that the Salvadoran government was gaining control of the military and the human rights situation was improving. Throughout the certification process that included congressional hearings, Elliot Abrams and other administration officials would deny the massacre by designing successful interpretive strategies for seemingly irrefutable evidence. The denial and the process by which the massacre was finally admitted offer lessons about how the horrors of war can be buried, even in plain sight. The massacre in the mountains of Morazan was brutal, well-planned, and totally unnecessary. A decade later, after the war could not be won by military means, peace was negotiated in a process that could easily have been achieved before tens of thousands of innocent civilians had been brutally murdered by security forces trained and supplied by the United States.

The Final Offensive and the Killing of the Jesuits Priests

As the war went on, so did the killing. By the end of the decade, under a renewed and fierce attack by the FMLN, an offensive that brought the war back into the streets of the capital, the Salvadoran army realized it would not be able to win a military victory. In desperation, security forces responded in their usual way, with atrocities and terror against civilians. But after all the killings, this time they would go too far.

Once again soldiers of the Atlacatl Brigade would take action. On November 16, 1989 dressed not in uniform, but in all black with stocking caps, they crept through the lush gardens of the campus of the Central American University and into the bedrooms of the Jesuit priests who lay sleeping. They would leave behind on the lawn outside the residence a scene of horrifying brutality. The bodies of six Jesuit priests, their cook, and her daughter lay on the blood-soaked grass where they had been dragged and shot execution style, but with so many bullets that little remained of their heads.

This terror would be the beginning of the end of the civil war. This time justifying more money for the generals would require an investigation. The U.S. Congress sent a team to El Salvador headed by Representative Joseph Moakley, a long-time congressman from

Massachusetts. Initial press reports followed what had through years of repetition become the entrenched convention, and statements by then U.S. Ambassador William Walker, that they did not know who killed the priests because "the history of atrocious death in El Salvador has come from extremes of both right and left." Yet on their first fact-finding trip, the congressman and his team quickly understood that the Salvadoran security forces had to be responsible for the murders.[43] Top military personnel lived in the same neighborhood where the Jesuits were killed and security forces had the area under constant surveillance. Through the course of his investigation, and because of his refusal to allow security forces to stonewall, Moakley and his task force discovered that the highest level of the Salvadoran military had been involved in the murders and had tried to cover up their actions.[44] Moakley reported the findings of the Task Force on the floor of the U.S. House of Representatives.

The United Nations helped broker a negotiated settlement that brought the war to an end in January 1992, after Salvadoran President Alfredo Christiani met with the comandantes of the FMLN. They signed a peace agreement called the Chapultepec Accords[45] that ended the 12-year civil war provided for a *commission on the truth* that would investigate "serious acts of violence that have occurred since 1980 and whose impact on society urgently demands that the public should know the truth."[46]

The Exhumation and the Truth Commission Report

The small convent that stood beside the church in the central square of El Mozote, the one that Alma Guillermoprieto referred to as the sacristy in the *Washington Post* a decade earlier, was exhumed in October and November 1992. Experienced Forensic Anthropologists from Argentine began their careful exhumation. They separated the splintered beams of the burnt building from the small bones and human fragments left of the children who had been gathered there and shot:

> In the laboratory, the skeletal remains of 143 bodies were identified, including 131 children under the age of 12, 5 adolescents and 7 adults. The experts noted in addition that, "the average age of the children was approximately 6 years of age."[47]

At the same level where the children's remains were found lay the empty shell casings of the Atlacatl Brigade carelessly left behind, and easy to discover had authorities been interested a decade earlier. Ballistic analysts found 245 cartridge cases, of which 184 had discernable headstamps, "identifying the ammunition as having been manufactured for the United States government at Lake City, Missouri." At least 24 people did the shooting with M-16 rifles, also manufactured in the United States. They stood inside, and at the doors and windows and shot in, and at least nine times in a downward angle, indicating the victims were on the floor. The evidence offers "full proof that the victims were summarily executed, as the witnesses have testified," and confirms the allegations that they were the intentional victims of an extra-judicial mass murder.

The Truth Commission also summarized the pattern of conduct by the military and its U.S. advisors. Counterinsurgency warfare, like Vietnam, was the most murderous on the civilian population. The Atlacatl, the Rapid Deployment Infantry Battalion carried out the massacre and was the first unit of its kind to be specially trained under the supervision of United States military advisers in early 1981.

Highly critical of the lack of prior investigation, the report states that the evidence shows "the collusion of senior commanders of the armed forces, for they show that the evidence of the unburied bodies was there for a long time for anyone who wanted to investigate the facts."[48] They rebuked the military for allowing the "deliberate, systematic and indiscriminate violence against the peasant population" that "went on for years." In addition to confirming the massacre at El Mozote, the Truth Commission also confirmed that the paramilitary death squads aligned with the Salvadoran military were responsible for 85 percent of the killings during the war.

Mark Danner published an account of the incident at El Mozote in his 1994 book, *The Massacre at El Mozote*. His work stands as a reckoning and tribute to the victims. Raymond Bonner continues to write about the massacre, the murder of the four church women, the situation in El Salvador, and the on-going efforts over the years to bring those accountable to justice.[49] He is presently working on a documentary film about the El Mozote Massacre.

Conclusion

On television, the real world, constituted through the movement of social forces and historical imperatives, was reduced to fragments, ripped out of context and rendered unintelligible—a baffling morass of "random violence." Media images of chaos and instability in El Salvador confirmed the public's worst fears of disorder and instability in the Third World. News and entertainment would mingle in ways that would increasingly blur fact from fiction, especially problematic for news from countries little known and not understood.

The media coverage of El Salvador in the 1980s continues to have a legacy of influence for both the media and the possibility for peace in the hemisphere. What we remember, or chose to forget of events in this region, tirelessly referred to as our own backyard, still affect political discourse and policy structures today.

The United States proved to be on the wrong side of history. This proxy war would result in another episode of horrific human rights violations, mostly forgotten in America, but remembered certainly by its victims, and now understood globally as part of America's history. In his final Sunday sermon, Archbishop Oscar Arnulfo Romero issued a plea to the country's military junta that continues to resonate today:

> In the name of God, in the name of this suffering people whose cries rise to heaven more loudly each day, I implore you, I beg you, I order you in the name of God: stop the repression.

The conflict in El Salvador would take the form of a bloody 12-year civil war that would cost the American taxpayers almost six billion dollars. What lessons does this episode teach about war and humanity? The nihilism of such violence is evidenced in the way the war finally came to an end—a negotiated peace deal brokered by the United Nations. After the war ended, funding from the United States went from tens of millions to tens of thousands and the country was left in shambles with almost no funding for restoration and rebuilding.[50] In the shadows of war, the gangs grew up to fill the vacant spaces where democratic institutions once stood. Refugees in the United States, traumatized by violence, lived in poverty in under-privileged neighborhoods in Los Angeles. In the 1980s, law enforcement strategies targeted low-income neighborhoods, and they ended up in the U.S. prison system, a point we will return to in Chapter 5. The military adventures perpetrated by the United States set in motion a cycle of violence in the hemisphere that is felt today and is the primary reason for the forced migrations from Central America. In Chapter 2, Adrian Bergmann details the resulting long-term humanitarian crisis that continues to play out in El Salvador today.

Notes

1 Liz Robbins, "Why was MS-13 Targeted in Trump's State of the Union Speech," *New York Times*, January 31, 2018, www.nytimes.com/2018/01/31/nyregion/ms-13-gang-trump.html
2 Ibid., Liz Robbins, 2018.
3 Caitlin Yelek, "Trump Mourns Mother of MS-13 Victim Killed at Daughter's Memorial Site," *Washington Examiner*, September 14, 2018, www.washingtonexaminer.com/news/trump-mourns-mother-of-ms-13-victim-killed-at-daughters-memorial-site
4 Liz Robbins, "Mother of Long Island Gang Victim Invited to the State of the Union," *New York Times*, January 28, 2019, www.nytimes.com/2018/01/28/nyregion/ms13-gang-long-island-murder.html
5 Jose Miguel Cruz, "Trump is Wrong About MS-13: His Rhetoric Will Make it Worse," *Washington Post*, January 31, 2018, www.washingtonpost.com/news/posteverything/wp/2018/01/31/trump-is-wrong-about-ms-13-and-his-rhetoric-will-make-it-worse/?utm_term=.179a37fb4f68
6 For a detailed discussion of forced migrations, the brutality of gangs in Central America, and their origins in the U.S., see Leighton Akio Woodhouse, "Running for their Lives," *The Intercept*, May 18, 2016, https://theintercept.com/2016/05/18/fleeing-gangs-central-american-refugees-fight-deportation-from-the-u-s/
7 Ibid., Liz Robbins, "Why was MS-13 Targeted in Trump's State of the Union Speech?" 2018.
8 The piece was published with *Newsday* and also featured on "This American Life" (whose story is separately a finalist for a Peabody Award). See *Pro-Publica*, "Pro-Publica and Partners Win Pulitzer Prize for MS-13 Coverage," April 15, 2019. www.propublica.org/article/pulitzer-winner-ms13-gangs-immigration-zero-tolerance
9 Ibid., *Pro-Publica*, 2019.
10 Much of the material in this chapter is the result of the author's analysis of the media coverage of the civil war in El Salvador much of which has been published in various formats over the years. It is based on early experiences in Central America, and media analysis as a graduate student. The most complete writings on the topic of media coverage of wars in Central America can be found in the book, *A Century of Media, A Century of War*, published by Perter Lang, 2006.
11 Christopher Dickey, *With the Contras: A Reporter in the Wilds of Central America* (New York: Simon and Schuster, 2008).
12 Andreas E. Feldmann and Maiju Perälä, "Reassessing the Causes of Non-governmental Terrorism in Latin America," *Latin American Politics and Society* 46, no. 2 (July 2004): 101–32, doi:10.1111/j.1548-2456.2004.tb00277.x. See also Noam Chomsky, *The Culture of Terrorism* (Montreal: Back Rose Books, 2008), 111, 130.
13 Greg Grandin and Gilbert Joseph, *A Century of Revolution: Insurgent and Counterinsurgent Violence during Latin America's Long Cold War* (Durham, NC: Duke University Press, 2010), 89.
14 Holly Sklar, *Washington's War on Nicaragua* (Boston, MA: South End Press, 1988), 70.
15 William M. Leo Grande, *Our Own Backyard: The United States in Central America, 1977–1992* (Chapel Hill: North Carolina Press, 2000).

16 Robert Perry and Peter Kornbluh, "Reagan's Pro-Contra Propaganda Machine," *Washington Post*, September 4, 1988, www.washingtonpost. com/archive/opinions/1988/09/04/reagans-pro-contra-propaganda-machine/42d256fc-9d93-4174-b629-06d91f9124c6/?utm_term=. 7a94e4110fd1

17 Edward Chamorro, *Packaging the Contras: The Case of CIA Disinformation*, Monograph Series 2 (New York: Institute for Media Analysis Inc., 1987). See also Robin Andersen, "Reagan's Public Diplomacy," *Covert Action Information Bulletin* 31 (1987): 20–4.

18 Ibid., Robert Perry and Peter Kornbluh, 1988.

19 See ibid., Robin Andersen, 2006, Chapter 9.

20 Leonard Downie and Robert Kaiser, *The News About the News: American Journalism in Peril* (New York: Alfred Knopf, 2002), 54.

21 Ibid., Robin Andersen, 2006, Chapter 5.

22 Robert Armstrong and Janet Shenk, *El Salvador: The Face of Revolution* (Boston, MA: South End Press, 1982), 122.

23 Mort Rosenblum, *Coups and Earthquakes* (New York: Harper & Row, 1979).

24 Americas Watch Committee and the American Civil Liberties Union, Report on Human Rights in El Salvador, (New York: Random House, 1982), 135.

25 Ibid., Armstrong and Shenk, 1982, 130.

26 Ibid., Americas Watch Committee and the American Civil Liberties Union, 1982.

27 Ibid., Americas Watch Committee and the American Civil Liberties Union, 1982.

28 Ibid., Americas Watch Committee and the American Civil Liberties Union, 1982.

29 Justin Wren-Lewis, "The Story of a Riot: the Television Cover of Civil Unrest in 1981," *Screen Education* 40 (1981–1982): 15.

30 Additionally, law and order news makes use of "a particular kind of narrative in which the disruption is unmotivated," Cary Bazalgette and Richard Paterson, "Reel Entertainment: The Iran Embassy Siege," *Screen Education* 37, Winter (1980–1981): 63.

31 Ibid., Wren-Lewis, 1981–1982, 16.

32 Ibid., Armstrong and Janet Shenk, 1982, 134.

33 Ibid., Armstrong and Janet Shenk, 1982, 135.

34 The Archbishop was interviewed shortly before his death, and these words appear on the documentary videotape "Enemies of War," 1999. Produced and Directed by Esther Cassidy.

35 Jon Lee Anderson, "Archbishop Óscar Romero Becomes a Saint, But His Death Still Haunts El Salvador," *The New Yorker*, October 22, 2018.

36 Ibid., Robin Andersen, 2006, Chapter 6.

37 Michael Massing, "About Face on El Salvador," *Columbia Journalism Review* 22 (November/December, 1983): 42–9.

38 Former *New York Times* reporter Chris Hedges tells of small pieces of paper stuffed inside the mouths of corpses addressed to journalists as a warning.

39 He was afraid they might be ambushed by the military, as four Dutch journalists would be two months later when they traveled with the guerrillas. I am indebted to Mark Danner for his excellent book, *The Massacre at El Mozote*, which I draw on heavily for this account.

40 Cited in Danner, 1994.

41 Cited in Danner, 1994, 101.

42 Alma Guillermoprieto, "Salvadoran Peasants Describe Mass Killing: Woman Tells of Children's Death," *Washington Post*, January 27, 1982.

43 Robert Pear, "Salvador Accused on Jesuit Inquiry," *New York Times*, May 1, 1990, www.nytimes.com/1990/05/01/world/salvador-accused-on-jesuit-inquiry.html

44 Among them, General Juan Bustillo, head of the Air Force, and General Emilio Ponce, Minister of Defense.

45 United Nations Peacemaker, Chapultepec Accords: SV_920116_ChapultepecAgreement.pdf

46 By November 1991, Tutela Legal, the Salvadoran human rights organization, had published the first comprehensive investigation of El Mozote and included on the list of those murdered where 794 names.

47 The report was originally published by the United Nations Security Council Annex, under the title, "El Salvador Agreements: The Path to Peace," DPI/1208, May 1992. It was also posted by United States Institute of Peace Library, under the title, "From Madness to Hope: The 12 year war in El Salvador, Report on the Commission of the Truth for El Salvador," S/25500, 1993, on January 26, 2001. ElSalvador-Report-1.pdf

48 It goes on to state: "In this case, we cannot accept the excuse that senior commanders knew nothing of what had happened."

49 See Raymond Bonner, "What Did Elliott Abrams have to do with the El Mozote Massacre," *The Atlantic*, February 15, 2019, www.theatlantic.com/ideas/archive/2019/02/ilhan-omar-elliott-abrams-and-el-mozote-massacre/582889/. See also Raymond Bonner, "The Diplomate and the Killer," *The Atlantic*, February 11, 2016, www.theatlantic.com/international/archive/2016/02/el-salvador-churchwomen-murders/460320/

50 Ibid., Enemies of War, 1999.

2 Violence, Migration, and the Perverse Effects of Gang Repression in Central America

Adrian Bergmann

Introduction

Over the course of 2015, one in every 970 Salvadorans was murdered—the highest rate of homicides per inhabitant recorded that year by any country in the world. Still, this is but the most radical expression of the chronic societal crisis that mars postwar El Salvador, Guatemala, and Honduras, with a plethora of violence wounding bodies and minds, human relationships, and communities.

Deep in the shadow of international terrorism and great power standoffs, and more than 20 years after the last peace accord was signed, El Salvador, Guatemala, and Honduras generally received scant concern or coverage in the international press, academia, and policy circles, and the humanitarian aspects of the regional security crisis is only of late receiving any significant attention.[1] The surge in the number of unaccompanied minors arriving to the United States from these three countries, and the kidnapping and presumed massacre of 43 students of the Ayotzinapa Rural Teachers' College in southern Mexico, served to put these issues on the agenda. By October 2015, the United Nations High Commissioner for Refugees warned of a "looming refugee crisis" in the region.[2]

Today, this public attention is largely driven by a narrative centered not on the humanitarian crisis in Central America, but on a crisis of unlawful immigration into the United States—although there is scant evidence to support the claim that such a crisis exists. Nevertheless, the U.S. federal government launched a series of efforts to "aggressively deter" potential immigrants and shift responsibility for keeping potential immigrants out of the United States to the governments of Central America and Mexico. Here, I ask whether the prevailing discourse may be reinforcing the dynamics of armed confrontation that are driving hundreds of thousands of Central Americans from their homes, toward a presumed safe haven in the United States.

Making the News: "Immigrants Have Overrun U.S. Border Security"

In early June 2014, Breitbart published a cache of photographs "depicting the conditions of foreign children warehoused by authorities on U.S. soil."[3] The accompanying article bemoaned that "thousands of illegal immigrants have overrun U.S. border security and their processing centers in Texas along the U.S./Mexico border," adding that "unaccompanied minors, including young girls under the age of 12, are making the dangerous journey from Central America and Mexico, through cartel-controlled territories, and across the porous border onto U.S. soil."

This coverage formed part of a flurry of media attention that catapulted the issue of immigration to the forefront of public conversation in the United States and set its tone: Starting in earnest in May 2014, outlets including Breitbart and Fox News spearheaded a narrative that "overwhelming" numbers of Central Americans were "flooding" into the country, driven by rumors that it was easy to gain entry into the United States, and that one would be able to stay.[4] Whether incidentally or by design, the idea that unlawful immigration was pushing the nation onto the brink thus marked the run-up to the U.S. mid-term elections in November 2014, forging a shift in policy orientation—especially among Republican lawmakers—from immigration reform to fighting against immigration. Five years on, immigration is still at the center of the political battleground in the United States, with the effects spilling back across the border into Mexico and Central America.

Before discussing the conditions that drive emigration from Central America, it is worth assessing whether there actually is a crisis of unlawful immigration into the United States. Three metrics go a long way to determine the real scale of the issue, namely the number of unlawful immigrants who (1) are apprehended, (2) successfully enter into the country, and (3) are deported. Data on each is recorded by the U.S. Department of Homeland Security (D.H.S.), an institution that can hardly be accused of pro-immigrant bias.

Firstly, as regards apprehensions, two federal agencies see to the enforcement of immigration laws in the United States, the U.S. Customs and Border Protection (C.B.P.) and the U.S. Immigration and Customs Enforcement (I.C.E.), both part of the D.H.S. In principle, the former focuses on enforcement at or near the country's borders, while the latter enforces immigration laws inside the United States. Between them, in 2014—the year that "overwhelming"

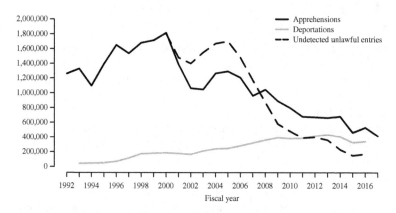

Figure 2.1 Apprehensions, deportations, and unlawful entries of immigrants to the United States.

Sources: Elaboration by the author with data from the United States Department of Homeland Security and of Justice. Office of Immigration Statistics, "Department of Homeland Security Border Security Metrics Report" (Washington, DC: Department of Homeland Security, 2018), www.dhs.gov/sites/default/files/publications/BSMR_OIS_2016.pdf; Office of Immigration Statistics, *Yearbook of Immigration Statistics*, National Serials Program (Washington, DC: United States Department of Homeland Security, 2002–2017), www.dhs.gov/immigration-statistics/yearbook; United States Immigration and Naturalization Service, *Statistical Yearbook of the Immigration and Naturalization Service*, National Serials Program (Washington, DC: United States Department of Justice, 1996–2001), www.dhs.gov/immigration-statistics/yearbook.

numbers of immigrants overran the "porous border"—the C.B.P. and I.C.E. apprehended some 680,000 "illegal aliens." Sure enough, that was a slight increase from the 662,000 apprehensions in 2013—but, then again, 2013 was the lowest year on record since 1973. As shown in Figure 2.1, the number of apprehensions subsequently dropped further in 2017, to 415,000, the lowest since 1970 and 77.1 percent lower than the peak of 1,815,000 in 2000.

Secondly, the falling number of apprehensions begs the question of whether more people are successfully entering the United States without being apprehended. According to the D.H.S., however, between fiscal years (F.Y.) 2006 and 2016, "estimated undetected unlawful entries fell from approximately 851,000 to nearly 62,000 ..., a 93 percent decrease."[5] In the same period, the "estimated probability of detection" of unlawful border crossers "increased from 70 percent in F.Y. 2006 ... to 91 percent in F.Y. 2016."[6]

Thirdly, the long-term trend is that far more Central Americans and others are being deported, first under the Illegal Immigration

Reform and Immigrant Responsibility Act of 1996 and, more strikingly, in the wake of the Homeland Security Act of 2002.

This is all to say that there have not been this few apprehensions of unlawful immigrants, this few undetected unlawful entries, and this high a probability of detection since at least the early 1970s. At the same time, ever more people are being deported. In line with these findings, a recent Pew Research Center study using census data concluded that, in 2016, the number of unauthorized immigrants living in the United States "is the lowest since 2004" and dropping.[7]

In other words, and as reflected in Figure 2.1, the overall scale of unlawful immigration into the United States is at a historic low. Even so, rather than challenge the false premises of the narrative of a crisis of unlawful immigration that exploded in 2014, the U.S. federal government rolled out policies geared at responding to the political crisis around immigration, rather than the driving forces behind immigration from Central America and Mexico, or the needs of refugees. Steeped within a securitized gaze, mainstream media did not provide the U.S. public with information that would serve to question the emphasis on law enforcement over other policy alternatives.

Responding to the News: "To Help Stem the Tide"

On June 2, 2014, Obama declared an "urgent humanitarian situation" in the Río Grande Valley in the southern border region.[8] Four weeks later, he reiterated the description in a letter to the U.S. Congress, only to call for "an aggressive deterrence strategy focused on the removal and repatriation of recent border crossers,"[9] the glaring contradiction between humanitarian urgency and aggressive deterrence notwithstanding. On the one hand, this policy gave way to further clamping down on both unlawful border crossers and undocumented immigrants within the United States. On the other, two key initiatives sought to move deterrence and enforcement outside the United States and away from its borders, namely the Southern Border Program and the Alliance for Prosperity.

Firstly, in July 2014, the Mexican government launched the Southern Border Program, aimed at stopping Central American migrants before they reach the United States. Only ten days after writing to the congressional leadership, Obama outlined in a speech how, "earlier this week, Mexico announced a series of steps that they're going to take on their southern border to help stem the tide of these unaccompanied children."[10] Sure enough, over the

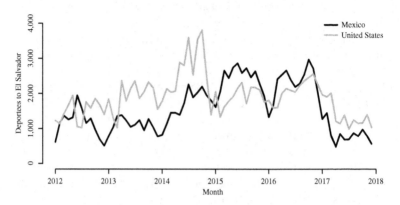

Figure 2.2 Monthly deportees to El Salvador by deporting country.
Source: Elaboration by the author with data from Salvadoran migration authorities. Dirección General de Migración y Extranjería, "Sistema Único de Información Migratoria" (San Salvador: Ministerio de Justicia y Seguridad Pública,
2018).

next four years—between July 1, 2014, and June 30, 2018—a little
over half a million Guatemalans, Hondurans, and Salvadorans
were deported by Mexican authorities.[11] As seen in Figure 2.2,
within months, Mexico surpassed the United States in terms of
the number of Salvadorans it deported, a situation that persisted
throughout 2015 and 2016.

Secondly, in January 2015, U.S. vice president Joseph R. Biden Jr.
announced the Alliance for Prosperity, a billion dollar aid package
for El Salvador, Guatemala, and Honduras, eventually cut back
by Congress to about 750 million. The primary condition for this
massive injection of capital into the small Central American states
is their active collaboration in implementing the aggressive deterrence strategy, while presumably overseeing "systemic change" at
home. In an op-ed in the *New York Times*, Biden asserted that, "as
we were reminded last summer when thousands of unaccompanied
children showed up on our southwestern border, the security and
prosperity of Central America are inextricably linked with our
own."[12] Ever since, the Alliance for Prosperity has served as a major incentive for Central American governments to seek to reduce
the outward flow of migrants.

In line with Biden's analysis, both the Southern Border Program and
the Alliance for Prosperity, as well as the broader aggressive deterrence
strategy, bundle together economic, humanitarian, immigration, and

security policy. That, though, is nothing new. Beyond the headlines of the past several years, the long-term dynamics of the transnational relationship between the United States and its neighbors to the south are key to understanding the response to the present crises, and go a long way toward explaining why that response may be informed as much by inadequate thinking about economics and security as the principles for humanitarian action or sound immigration policy. For the better part of two decades, security policy in general and gang policy in particular has played an important role in shaping that relationship,[13] as well as the political arenas in the Central American states themselves. El Salvador serves here as a case study.

Electoral Politics of Security: "How the Street Gangs Took Central America"

Analyses of media discourses and public policies on crime, youth, and gangs show that the run-ups to the 1999 and especially 2004 presidential elections were central to the shift from seeing gangs as a social issue among many to a key security issue in El Salvador.[14] In the tightly fought 2004 vote, outgoing president Francisco Flores of the National Republican Alliance (ARENA) put gang policy front and center, as he launched a massive campaign of repression directed at gangs, commonly known as "mano dura." It included a wave of discretionary arrests, constriction of due process guarantees, and increased participation of the military in policing.[15] The policy would become a cornerstone of ARENA candidate Antonio Saca's successful bid for the presidency, and similar policies were introduced in Guatemala and Honduras at around the same time.

Alisha Holland argues that rendering gangs as a grave and urgent threat to society served to overcome tensions within ARENA, and to consolidate a voter base by using gang policy to drive a wedge between ARENA and the main opposition party, the Farabundo Martí Front for National Liberation (FMLN), which protested the new policy.[16] Similarly, Sonja Wolf[17] contends that "Mano Dura was a punitive, populist move designed to enhance the electoral appeal of ARENA rather than to mitigate the gang problem." Ever since, gang policy has been a key campaign issue for any party.

When Wolf reviewed 2,874 news items concerning gangs in El Salvador's two main newspapers between 2003 and 2006, she found that "the press played a key role in selling the supposed effectiveness of suppression, chiefly by turning Mano Dura into a spectacle and publishing indicators of policy success."[18] Furthermore, she concluded that, "rather than disclosing and challenging the human rights violations and a priori convictions of supposed offenders, the media were complicit in their occurrence."[19]

Foreign media and scholars, along with U.S. government and law enforcement officials, largely got behind this framing of gangs as a threat and an enemy, and that violent repression was the right response. Sensationalist examples include *Foreign Affairs*' publication of Ana Arana's "How the Street Gangs Took Central America" and National Geographic Channel's broadcast of "World's Most Dangerous Gang,"[20] while the Federal Bureau of Investigations pushed to set up anti-gang task forces in Central America.

What is more, on the heels of the invasion of Iraq, a group of scholars linked to the U.S. Army War College set out to apply the lens of urban counterinsurgency to Central America, yielding treats such as Max G. Manwaring's observation that if gangs such as the 18th Street and the Mara Salvatrucha "look like ducks, walk like ducks, and act like ducks—they indeed are insurgent-type ducks."[21] More recently, journalist Douglas Farah saw fit to claim that the Mara Salvatrucha "is actively looking" to learn from groups such as al-Qaeda and the Islamic State of Iraq and the Levant,[22] on the feeble grounds that police found evidence of internet searches about these groups on one gang member's computer. When it comes to Central American gangs, it seems like no claim is too outrageous.

Today, the myths surrounding gangs live on, and are mobilized in the political crisis around immigration in the United States. In the midst of the flurry of attention and political wrangling over the "caravans" of Central American migrants, beginning in October 2018, and in the lead-up to the U.S. mid-term elections, *The Wall Street Journal* reported on El Salvador as beset by a "new breed of gangs."[23] Readers let on their reactions in the online comment section about these "savages," the "subhuman group who has not evolved," the "barbarians," and this "truly frightening subspecies of man." This is a narrative that draws upon widespread repertoires of dehumanization,[24] and one that has been cultivated about young men in Central America for a long time.[25] Gradually, they have come to serve as justification for approaches to "security" that play on the politics of fear and demand militarized responses to issues that might better be understood and addressed as social issues. Instead, though, the current political and media climate is drawing upon and further entrenching these discourses.

At the same time, over the four years since the summer of unaccompanied children, economic, migration, and security policy have continued to be conflated. Obama's successor, Donald J. Trump, has threatened to cut financial aid to Central American states, called for legislative reforms to suppress immigrants, and dispatched more than 5,000 military troops to the U.S. southern border to confront the caravans.[26] This followed Trump's denunciation that the ragtag bands of Central American migrants constitute "an invasion of our Country," warning that "our Military is waiting for you!"[27]

How might we better understand the decisions of hundreds of thousands of Central Americans each year who embark on journey with the hope of settling in the United States?

Perverse Development Drives Migration

There is a long tradition of emigration from El Salvador, Guatemala, and Honduras to the United States, and extensive social and economic bonds have developed in its wake. First, an important component of these transnational relationships is personal remittances, which today account for around 20 percent of gross domestic product in El Salvador and Honduras, and a little over half of that in Guatemala, as exhibited in Figure 2.3. This makes remittances immensely important to the Central American political economies, and to millions of Central Americans.[28]

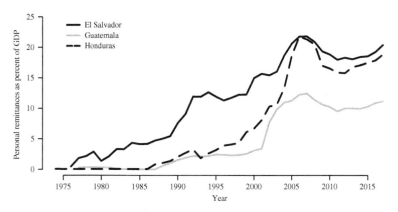

Figure 2.3 Personal remittances received, as percent of gross domestic product.

Source: Elaboration by the author with data from World Bank. World Bank, "Personal Remittances, Received (% of GDP)," BX.TRF.PWKR.DT.GD.ZS (Washington, DC: World Bank, 2018), https://data.worldbank.org/indicator/bx.trf.pwkr.dt.gd.zs.

As Aaron Schneider points out, "the sheer number of migrants raises questions about a development model that expels people from their homes, exports them and their labour to other countries, and then depends on their foreign exchange to balance the macroeconomy."[29] Over the past several decades, the economies of the Central American societies have undergone massive shifts,[30] and remittances may be best understood as "a side-effect of the massive dislocations provoked by economic transformation"[31]—that is, a strategy for individuals and families to adapt to their economic realities.

Second, another key driver of emigration is social relationships, as ever more Central Americans have family members living abroad, and migration is a way of maintaining the bonds.[32] The Bureau of the Census estimated that some 815,000 Guatemalan, 623,000 Honduran, and 1,391,000 Salvadoran immigrants were living in the United States in 2017, out of a total immigrant population of around 44,556,000.[33] Those numbers are equivalent to 4.8, 6.7, and 21.8 percent, respectively, of the populations living inside these three countries, making the relative scale of this driver of emigration especially significant for El Salvador.

Internal Displacement: "A Hidden Tragedy and Publicly Unacknowledged Crisis"

Over the past few years, however, the question of why people emigrate has been asked anew, amid increased awareness of the humanitarian consequences of organized armed violence in El Salvador, Guatemala, and Honduras. A key manifestation of this humanitarian crisis is forced displacement within and across borders,[34] an issue that observers have been slow to acknowledge, perhaps owing to its low visibility. As David James Cantor points out,

> in contrast with conflict-displacement scenarios such as Colombia, where the dynamics of the armed confrontation have sometimes produced highly visible mass displacement of entire sectors or villages, forced displacement due to gang violence in the Northern Triangle [El Salvador, Guatemala, and Honduras] is largely invisible to outside observers.[35] This is a displacement that usually takes place *gota-a-gota* (drop by drop), person-by-person, family-by-family ....[36]

In 2016, I spoke with a couple right after they had driven home at night through a residential neighborhood in San Salvador.

The streets were mostly empty and only one other car was in sight, heading in the same direction as the couple. It stopped and they came to a stop behind it. Without stepping out of their vehicle, the occupants of first car fired a handful of bullets at a house by the side of the road, and then drove off. The stunned couple also drove off, in a different direction, and drove around for a little while before going home, worried that the shooters might have decided to follow them. On a Saturday morning, two weeks later, I happened to walk past the house that had been shot at, as its contents were packed into a moving van under police watch. It seemed a completely mundane scene—nothing out of the ordinary. Had I not known what had happened two weeks earlier, I would have been none the wiser as to the presumable cause of their move.

The United Nations Special Rapporteur on the Human Rights of Internally Displaced Persons, Cecilia Jiménez-Damary,[37] emphasized similar dynamics during a visit to El Salvador in September 2017, concluding that "the extraordinary violence and internal displacement that it causes is a hidden tragedy and publicly unacknowledged crisis." While 30 years earlier, whole neighborhoods and villages were forced to uproot and leave together—collective experiences with violence and displacement during wars and military dictatorships—today's tragedies and dramas are increasingly individualized, privatized experiences.[38]

All the while, the scale of forced displacement is inherently difficult to estimate, given that victims seek to avoid attention and detection. Furthermore, the lack of specialized services, not to mention public confidence in state institutions, means that few Central Americans inform the authorities about their predicament. In a particularly succinct conclusion, Jiménez-Damary's predecessor, Chaloka Beyani,[39] reported in April 2016 that, in Honduras, "a lack of resources and attention means that most internally displaced persons are left to fend for themselves." In his assessment, "internally displaced persons are not provided with the protection and support to which they are entitled and immigration and asylum policies and practices fail to live up to international standards required for those fleeing violence or persecution." In El Salvador, the authorities have not even fully recognized the phenomenon of internal forced displacement, referring instead of "internal mobility due to violence."[40]

Given the paucity of evidence, journalists, academics, and state authorities alike have attempted to gauge the number of people affected. While their efforts are presumably well-intentioned, they often yield misleading results. For instance, the Internal Displacement Monitoring Centre estimated that "up to 288,900" people were internally displaced in El Salvador in 2014.[41] This estimate, though, was extrapolated from a mere 57 respondents who said "yes" when asked in a survey of 1,246 people if they had changed their place of residence over the course of the past year due to receiving threats.[42] In other words, a single yes represented more than 5,000 people; one more no, and 5,000 people would be shaved off the estimate. In stark contrast, in a survey of 41,650 families from 20 municipalities where relatively more cases of forced displacement were expected to have taken place, only 466 cases were identified to have taken place during the whole of the period from 2006 to 2016.[43] The methodologies were completely different and generated radically different findings, ultimately providing little insight into the scale of internal displacement but underlining the importance of acknowledging and openly discussing methodological weaknesses, and, not least, the particular challenges of survey research in these contexts.

Violence and the Need for International Protection

Contrary to internally displaced persons, migrants that cross international borders are generally easier to monitor, and one category in particular is carefully registered, namely those who apply for asylum under international law. As shown in Figure 2.4, the rate of asylum-seekers from El Salvador, Guatemala, and Honduras has increased sharply since 2014, with 96 percent of their applications for protection between 2012 and 2017 being presented in the United States.

To put this Central American crisis in global context, in 2017, a staggering one in every 106 Salvadorans applied for asylum abroad, making for the second highest rate of asylum-seekers in the world, as seen in Figure 2.5. That year, Honduras ranked sixth and Guatemala fourteenth, making the "looming refugee crisis" that the U.N. High Commissioner for Refugees warned about two years earlier a matter of fact.

It is extremely difficult to determine what mix of motivations is currently driving hundreds of thousands of Central Americans to leave their homelands every year. People rarely decide to up their lives, make a costly and perilous journey, and settle in another country for a single, straightforward reason, but rather a set of individual circumstances that makes emigration seem like the better decision for one's own life and the lives of loved ones.

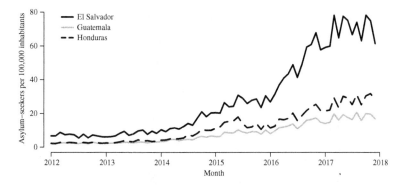

Figure 2.4 Monthly rate of asylum-seekers by country of origin.

Sources: Elaboration by the author with asylum data from the United Nations High Commissioner for Refugees and population data the United Nations Department of Economic and Social Affairs. Field Information and Coordination Support Section, "Population Statistics Database" (Geneva: United Nations High Commissioner for Refugees, 2018), https://popstats.unhcr.org; Population Division, "World Population Prospect: The 2017 Revision" (New York: United Nations Department of Economic and Social Affairs, 2017), https://population.un.org/wpp/DVD/Files/1_Indicators%20(Standard)/EXCEL_FILES/1_Population/WPP2017_POP_F01_1_TOTAL_POPULATION_BOTH_SEXES.xlsx.

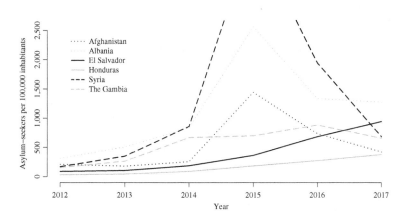

Figure 2.5 Countries with the highest rates of asylum-seekers in 2017.

Sources: Elaboration by the author with asylum data from the United Nations High Commissioner for Refugees and population data from the World Bank. Field Information and Coordination Support Section, "Population Statistics Database"; World Bank, "Population, Total," SP.POP.TOTL (Washington, DC: World Bank, 2018), https://data.worldbank.org/indicator/sp.pop.totl.

Note: In 2015, Syria reached a rate of 4,170 asylum-seekers per 100,000 inhabitants.

Undoubtedly, the economic and social drivers of emigration from Central America noted above remain important, but the need for protection has also gained greater importance.

To this effect, Jonathan T. Hiskey et al. have examined the emigration decisions of Guatemalans, Hondurans, and Salvadorans in 2014. Drawing upon a combination of national and subnational surveys, they find that citizens from El Salvador and Honduras who reported having been victims of violent crime were significantly more likely to consider emigration than those who had not had such traumatic experiences, and the likelihood increased if they had been victims of violent crime several times. Hence Hiskey et al. conclude that, "whereas victimization does not appear to influence the emigration calculus among Guatemalans, it is among the most important factors in predicting whether or not a Salvadoran or Honduran will report intentions to emigrate."[44]

Certainly, direct personal experiences with violent crime is not the only source of trauma or a need for protection. Presumably, the Central Americans who apply for asylum abroad do so not so much because of past experiences but due to the threat of injury or death if they had remained in their homeland. Herein lies a central paradox for those whose task it is to make the case for an individual's application for asylum: How to provide evidence to substantiate that someone has "credible fear" that something which has not yet happened might happen?

The Fallout of Repression

The ability to consider complexity in emigration decisions corresponds to the complexity in the scenario of fear and violence across Central America and Mexico. To give just one illustration of this, Figure 2.6 shows the homicide rate across the hundreds of municipalities of Belize, El Salvador, Guatemala, and Honduras for the year 2015. The diversity of experience is evident, with striking differences between the Guatemalan highlands in the west, to the great cities of Honduras—El Progreso, San Pedro Sula, Tegucigalpa—to the metropolitan area of San Salvador and communities along the eastern coast of El Salvador.

There is an important information gap about what particular drivers are, at different moments, relatively more important for different groups of migrants. Significantly, we know very little about the asylum-seekers—only their sex, age, and country of origin, but not where within the country or under what conditions each

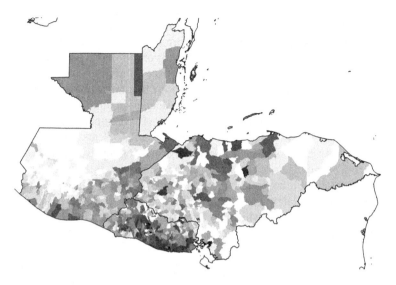

Figure 2.6 Homicides per inhabitant by municipality in 2015.
Sources: Elaboration by the author with data from the Belize Crime Observatory, Diálogos for Guatemala, the Public Prosecutor's Office for Honduras, and the Supreme Court of Justice for El Salvador. Belize Crime Observatory, "Homicide Count and Rate (2009–2017)" (Belize: National Security Council Secretariat, 2018), http://crimeobservatory.bz/docstation/com_docstation/44/bco_homicide_rate_by_district2009_2017_oct2018.xlsx; Carlos A. Mendoza and Sergio Zapeta, "Datos sobre la violencia homicida en Guatemala: anuales y municipales por tipo de arma utilizada por los victimarios del año 2001 al año 2017" (Guatemala: Diálogos, 2018), www.dialogos.org.gt/wp-content/uploads/2018/10/PNC-tasas-anuales-de-homicidios-2001-al-2017-por-tipo-de-arma-o-causa-MUNICIPAL.xlsx; Unidad de Acceso a la Información Pública, UAIP/2788/RR/195/2018(2) (San Salvador: Corte Suprema de Justicia, February 6, 2018); Unidad de Acceso a la Información Pública, SOL-MP-392-2019 (Tegucigalpa: Ministerio Público, February 12, 2019).

person left. However, it is reasonable to expect that fear of harm will be a stronger driver in the areas of Central America where armed violence is most acutely focused. Nuance and complexity, though, seem like lost virtues in the media coverage and political battle over both immigration to the United States and security policy in Central America.

A puzzling development in recent years is that many journalists and advocates for the rights of migrants and asylum-seekers have found a degree of common cause in exploiting the extreme depictions of Central American insecurity in general, and gang members in particular.[45] On the face of it, it is a framing of the issue that sells the news, and one that helps to win asylum cases. Of course, many of these depictions are true to reality, and reflect the deep human trauma that is festering in communities across these countries. However, a side effect of stressing the extreme threat of gang and drug cartel violence is that it feeds into the kinds of repressive policies that have been driving the cycles of violence over the past two decades.[46]

One person that has leaned heavily into this narrative is Trump. When he announced his bid for the presidency in June 2015, he bemoaned that "when Mexico sends its people, they're not sending their best. ... They're sending people that have lots of problems, and they're bringing those problems with us. They're bringing drugs. They're bringing crime. They're rapists."[47] In the same vein, in May 2018, he said of unlawful immigrants that "these aren't people. These are animals."[48] Months later, well into the 2018 mid-term campaign, Trump gave another speech, in which he stated that "a vote for any Democrat in November is a vote to eliminate immigration enforcement, to open our borders and set loose vicious predators and violent criminals," and warning that "they will be preying on our communities."[49] To the extent that this narrative shapes U.S. immigration policy, not to mention U.S. security cooperation with El Salvador, Guatemala, Honduras, and Mexico, it is reason for grave concern. However, as we have seen above, this is a narrative that finds echo in Central America.

Over the years, the demonization of gang members and the dynamics of violent confrontation between gangs and state security forces in El Salvador and Honduras has become ever more entrenched, with a dual effect of further deepening the security crisis and blocking the kinds of policies that might lead toward a different future. Again, El Salvador serves as an illustration.

Toward a Politics of Violence Reduction

When ARENA lost the Salvadoran presidential elections to the FMLN in 2009, after 20 years of continuous rule, the new president, Mauricio Funes, would come to oversee several dramatic and contradictory shifts in gang policy. The FMLN had long advocated a more progressive and comprehensive approach to dealing with insecurity, emphasizing its roots in social injustice, and expectations were very high. During the first two and a half years in government, though, disappointment grew as results were more evident in terms of reform and strengthening of the institutions in the justice and public sector, than in terms of people's lived experience on the streets and in their homes. A more hardline approach was announced with president Funes's appointment of general

David Munguía Payés as Minister of Justice and Public Security in November 2011. However, within a few, intense months, another dramatic turn had been made.

The public would come to know of it on March 14, 2012, through a publication of the Salvadoran online magazine *El Faro*, under the headline "Government Negotiates Reduction in Homicides with Gangs:" The article informed its readers that "last week, between Thursday and Saturday, around 30 gang members, leaders of the Mara Salvatrucha and Barrio 18, were moved from El Salvador's maximum-security prison to less secure jails. ... The transfers were part of a pact between the gangs and the Salvadoran government."[50] The agreement had been worked out over the preceding weeks, and stipulated that the gangs ensure a stiff reduction in homicides—which they did. Literally from one day to the next, the number of homicides in El Salvador dropped by half, and the drop would be sustained for well over a year before starting to creep up again.[51]

At least two conditions were crucial to the effectiveness of this homicide reduction strategy, widely known as "the truce." On the one hand, over the preceding decade, the main gangs in El Salvador had achieved a high degree of internal cohesion and effective organization.[52] Unlike in Guatemala and Honduras, this allowed a fairly small group of gang leaders to pull the rank and file along on a path of negotiations. On the other hand, while the government's public position on the truce was highly contradictory, its practical support was indispensable.[53]

What developed over more than a year into a full-fledged, gang-led peace process served as a forceful demonstration that "key stakeholders have the capacity to renegotiate existing norms of violence and that at least some gangs have the capacity to exert substantial informal social control over their members that can result in reduced violence."[54] Gradually, however, the process unraveled, and the reasons for that are important to understand and learn from.[55]

While there was no clear-cut moment at which the truce was over, and the renewed increase in homicides was slow, it is clear that the underlying politics of peace making crumbled. The truce had defied both popular opinion and the long-standing, official line of non-engagement with gangs, but the unprecedented homicide reduction afforded gang leaders, mediators, and state sponsors some time and room to maneuver. That time, however, would run out. As the 2014 elections drew closer, the window of opportunity was definitively closed, with all political parties—including the FMLN—swearing never to "negotiate with terrorists."

The Return of the Iron Fist

In an interview in late 2015, chief mediator Raúl Mijango looked back at the truce and lamented that "the political factor is the one that can do the most damage to any action that seeks to resolve the problem of violence. Why? Because the [political] parties, in a spectrum as polarized as the Salvadoran one, always want to make political gains."[56] That is to say that, although the truce made a dramatic break with established policy, it did not substantially alter the political and electoral dynamics that surround gangs—and certainly not their role in the transnational relationship between Central America, Mexico, and the United States.

In an incisive analysis of security policy during the 2009–2014 presidency, which puts the truce in context, Chris van der Borgh and Wim Savenije remark that, "while some types of dialogue [with gangs] seem to be unavoidable, such a strategy is extremely unpopular among many relevant audiences and therefore difficult to communicate publicly."[57] As such, the challenge extended well beyond changing party and electoral politics. Ultimately, the truce's sponsors failed to establish its legitimacy as a homicide reduction strategy in the eyes of large sections of the Salvadoran public, and were thus unable to garner the support necessary to sustain and strengthen any processes of broader, negotiated change. The difficulty of communicating effectively through domestic media was part and parcel of this failure.[58] Crucially, the media failed to provide readers, listeners, and viewers with a language that might have allowed for a meaningful policy discussion—a way of imagining a future with less violence, but acknowledging that gangs are not going away.

The collapse of the truce gave way to a radicalized return to repressive policies, leading the U.N. High Commissioner for Human Rights, Zeid Ra'ad Al Hussein, to decry the implementation a collection of draconian measures on prisoners for having "placed thousands of people in prolonged and isolated detention under truly inhumane conditions."[59] Following a massive increase in homicides committed by law enforcement officers, U.N. Special Rapporteur on Extrajudicial, Arbitrary, or Summary Executions, Agnés Callamard, denounce "a pattern of behaviour amongst security personnel, amounting to extrajudicial executions and excessive use of force, which is fed by very weak institutional responses."[60] In tune with the transnational convergence on securitizing migrants, Salvadoran politicians also passed legislation "for the control and follow-up of the returning Salvadoran population designated as members of maras, gangs, or illicit groups"[61]—a murky designation, at best.

Conclusion

Currently, U.S. policy toward Central America is a tangled mess whereby immigration policy is packaged with economic policy, humanitarian policy, and security policy. A precondition for making progress on these issues is to recognize that, contrary to the prevailing discourse, there are fewer unlawful immigrants entering the United States, and more of those who enter are deported, than at any time in recorded history. Over the past 15 years, this has in fact led to a decrease in the number of unlawful immigrants living in the United States.

Even so, hundreds of thousands of Central Americans do indeed make their way northward every year, due to the extensive transnational economic and social bonds that have developed over recent decades, as well as a chronic crisis of violence. Of late, though, also those who seek to exercise their "right to seek and to enjoy in other countries asylum from persecution" under article 14 of the Universal Declaration of Human Rights are faced with repression upon arrival at the United States' southern border,[62] generating an actual humanitarian crisis in the border regions. This constitutes yet another extension of ongoing efforts to deter potential migrants. All the while, much of the responsibility for keeping potential immigrants out of the United States has been shifted to the governments of Central America and Mexico, promoting the conflation between security, migration, and humanitarian issues also in this region.

The prescribed cures for the crises of refugees, security, and economics seem to be about as harmful as the original illnesses. Although the experiences in El Salvador, Guatemala, and Honduras differ greatly from one another, the predominantly repressive approaches to tackling armed violence consistently reinforces the dynamics of armed confrontation that are driving hundreds of thousands of Central Americans from their homes.

Notes

1 David James Cantor, "The New Wave: Forced Displacement Caused by Organized Crime in Central America and Mexico," *Refugee Survey Quarterly* 33, no. 3 (2014): 34–68, https://doi.org/10.1093/rsq/hdu008; Internal Displacement Monitoring Centre, "New Humanitarian Frontiers: Addressing Criminal Violence in Mexico and Central America" (Geneva: Norwegian Refugee Council, 2016); Nicolás Rodríguez Serna, "Fleeing Cartels and *Maras*: International Protection Considerations and Profiles from the Northern Triangle," *International Journal of Refugee Law* 28, no. 1 (2016): 25–54, https://doi.org/10.1093/ijrl/eev061.

2 United Nations High Commissioner for Refugees, *Women on the Run: First-Hand Accounts of Refugees Fleeing El Salvador, Guatemala, Honduras, and Mexico*, ed. Chiara Cardoletti-Carroll, Alice Farmer, and Leslie E. Vélez (Washington, DC: United Nations High Commissioner for Refugees, 2015), 49, www.unhcr.org/5630f24c6.pdf

3 Brandon Darby, "Leaked Images Reveal Children Warehoused in Crowded U.S. Cells, Border Patrol Overwhelmed," Breitbart, June 5, 2014, www.breitbart.com/texas/2014/06/05/leaked-images-reveal-children-warehoused-in-crowded-us-cells-border-patrol-overwhelmed/

4 Kristin Tate, "Go to America with Your Child, You Won't Get Turned Away," Breitbart, June 5, 2014, www.breitbart.com/texas/2014/06/05/go-to-america-with-your-child-you-wont-get-turned-away/

5 Office of Immigration Statistics, "Department of Homeland Security Border Security Metrics Report," 13.

6 Ibid., 18.

7 Jeffrey S. Passel and D'Vera Cohn, "U.S. Unauthorized Immigration Total Lowest in a Decade" (Washington, DC: Pew Research Center, November 27, 2018), 16, www.pewhispanic.org/wp-content/uploads/sites/5/2018/11/Pew-Research-Center_U.S.-Unauthorized-Immigrants-Total-Dips_2018-11-27.pdf

8 Katie Zezima and Ed O'Keefe, "Obama Calls Surge of Children across U.S.-Mexican Border 'Urgent Humanitarian Situation,'" *Washington Post*, June 2, 2014, www.washingtonpost.com/politics/obama-calls-wave-of-children-across-us-mexican-border-urgent-humanitarian-situation/2014/06/02/4d29df5e-ea8f-11e3-93d2-edd4be1f5d9e_story.html

9 Barack Obama to John Boehner et al., "Efforts to Address the Humanitarian Situation in the Rio Grande Valley Areas of Our Nation's Southwest Border," June 30, 2014, https://obamawhitehouse.archives.gov/the-press-office/2014/06/30/letter-president-efforts-address-humanitarian-situation-rio-grande-valle

10 Barack Obama, "Statement by the President on Immigration," July 9, 2014, https://obamawhitehouse.archives.gov/the-press-office/2014/07/09/statement-president-immigration

11 Unidad de Política Migratoria, "Boletín Mensual de Estadísticas Migratorias" (City of Mexico: Secretaría de Gobernación, 2012–2018), www.politicamigratoria.gob.mx/es_mx/SEGOB/Boletines_Estadisticos

12 Joseph R. Biden, "A Plan for Central America," *New York Times*, January 29, 2015, sec. Opinion Pages.

13 Elana Zilberg, *Space of Detention: The Making of a Transnational Gang Crisis between Los Angeles and San Salvador* (Durham, NC: Duke University Press, 2011).

14 Mo Hume, "*Mano Dura*: El Salvador Responds to Gangs," *Development in Practice* 17, no. 6 (2007): 739–51, https://doi.org/10.1080/09614520701628121; Roxana Martel Trigueros, "Las maras salvadoreñas: nuevas formas de espanto y control social," *Estudios Centroamericanos* 61, no. 696 (2006): 957–79; Amparo Marroquín Parducci, "En la república de la muerte: reflexiones en torno a las coberturas periodísticas sobre violencia en el Triángulo Norte de Centroamérica," in *Delincuencia, juventud y sociedad: materiales para reflexión*, ed. Mario Zetino Duarte (San

Salvador: Facultad Latinoamericana de Ciencias Sociales, 2011), 127–50; Irene Vasilachis de Gialdino, "Representations of Young People Associated with Crime in El Salvador's Written Press," *Critical Discourse Studies* 4, no. 1 (2007): 1–28, https://doi.org/10.1080/17405900601149400

15 Elizabeth Fuentes, "Legislación antipandillas y planes mano dura: ¿un derecho penal del enemigo?," in *Violencia en tiempos de paz: conflictividad y criminalización en El Salvador*, ed. Óscar Meléndez and Adrian Bergmann (San Salvador: Secretaría de Cultura de la Presidencia, 2015), 115–46.

16 Alisha C. Holland, "Right on Crime? Conservative Party Politics and *Mano Dura* Policies in El Salvador," *Latin American Research Review* 48, no. 1 (2013): 44–67, https://doi.org/10.1353/lar.2013.0009

17 Sonja Wolf, *Mano Dura: The Politics of Gang Control in El Salvador* (Austin: University of Texas Press, 2017), 4.

18 Sonja Wolf, "Creating Folk Devils: Street Gang Representations in El Salvador's Print Media," *Journal of Human Security* 8, no. 2 (2012): 52.

19 Wolf, 53.

20 Ana Arana, "How the Street Gangs Took Central America," *Foreign Affairs* 84, no. 3 (2005): 98–110; Marc Shaffer, "World's Most Dangerous Gang," *National Geographic Explorer* (Washington, DC: National Geographic Channel, February 12, 2006).

21 Max G. Manwaring, *Street Gangs: The New Urban Insurgency* (Carlisle, PA: U.S. Army War College, 2005), 33, http://purl.access.gpo.gov/GPO/LPS62132

22 Douglas Farah, "Central America's Gangs Are All Grown Up," *Foreign Policy*, January 19, 2016, https://foreignpolicy.com/2016/01/19/central-americas-gangs-are-all-grown-up/

23 Robbie Whelan, "Why Are People Fleeing Central America? A New Breed of Gangs Is Taking Over," *The Wall Street Journal*, November 2, 2018, www.wsj.com/articles/pay-or-die-extortion-economy-drives-latin-americas-murder-crisis-1541167619

24 Daniel Bar-Tal, Neta Oren, and Rafi Nets-Zehngut, "Sociopsychological Analysis of Conflict-Supporting Narratives: A General Framework," *Journal of Peace Research* 51, no. 5 (2014): 662–75, https://doi.org/10.1177/0022343314533984; Susan Opotow, "Moral Exclusion and Injustice: An Introduction," *Journal of Social Issues* 46, no. 1 (1990): 1–20, https://doi.org/10.1111/j.1540-4560.1990.tb00268.x

25 Sebastian Huhn, "Questioning the Crime Wave: On the Rise of Punitive Populism in Central America since the 1950s," in *Politics and History of Violence and Crime in Central America*, ed. Sebastian Huhn and Hannes Warnecke-Berger (New York: Palgrave Macmillan, 2017), 113–46, https://doi.org/10.1057/978-1-349-95067-6_5; Peter Peetz, "Youth Violence in Central America: Discourses and Policies," *Youth & Society* 43, no. 4 (2011): 1459–98, https://doi.org/10.1177/0044118X10384236

26 Nancy A. Youssef and Alicia A. Caldwell, "Trump to Deploy 5,200 Troops to Southern Border," *Wall Street Journal*, October 30, 2018, www.wsj.com/articles/military-to-deploy-5-000-troops-to-southern-border-u-s-officials-say-1540820650

27 Jordan Fabian, "Trump: Migrant Caravan 'Is an Invasion,'" *The Hill*, October 29, 2018, https://thehill.com/homenews/administration/413624-trump-calls-migrant-caravan-an-invasion

28 David Pedersen, *American Value: Migrants, Money, and Meaning in El Salvador and the United States* (Chicago, IL: University of Chicago Press, 2013).
29 Aaron Schneider, "The Great Transformation in Central America: Transnational Accumulation and the Evolution of Capital," in *Handbook of Central American Governance*, ed. Diego Sánchez-Ancochea and Salvador Martí i Puig (London: Routledge, 2014), 34; see also Sarah Gammage, "Exporting People and Recruiting Remittances: A Development Strategy for El Salvador?," *Latin American Perspectives* 33, no. 6 (2006): 75–100, https://doi.org/10.1177/0094582X06294112
30 Benedicte Bull, Fulvio Castellacci, and Yuri Kasahara, *Business Groups and Transnational Capitalism in Central America: Economic and Political Strategies* (Basingstoke: Palgrave Macmillan, 2014), https://doi.org/10.1057/9781137359407; William I. Robinson, *Transnational Conflicts: Central America, Social Change, and Globalization* (London: Verso, 2003).
31 Schneider, "The Great Transformation in Central America," 33.
32 Lauren Heidbrink, *Migrant Youth, Transnational Families, and the State: Care and Contested Interests* (Philadelphia: University of Pennsylvania Press, 2014).
33 Bureau of the Census, "Current Population Survey: Annual Social and Economic Supplement, 2017" (Washington, DC: United States Department of Commerce, 2018).
34 United Nations High Commissioner for Refugees, *Children on the Run: Unaccompanied Children Leaving Central America and Mexico and the Need for International Protection*, ed. Pamela Goldberg (Washington, DC: United Nations High Commissioner for Refugees, 2014), www.unhcr.org/56fc266f4.pdf; United Nations High Commissioner for Refugees, *Women on the Run*.
35 Cantor, "The New Wave," 52–61.
36 David James Cantor, "As Deadly as Armed Conflict? Gang Violence and Forced Displacement in the Northern Triangle of Central America," *Agenda Internacional* 23, no. 34 (2016): 89, https://doi.org/10.18800/agenda.201601.003
37 Cecilia Jiménez-Damary, "Report of the Special Rapporteur on the Human Rights of Internally Displaced Persons on Her Visit to El Salvador," A/HRC/38/39/Add.1 (Geneva: United Nations Human Rights Council, April 23, 2018), 16.
38 Ellen Moodie, *El Salvador in the Aftermath of Peace: Crime, Uncertainty, and the Transition to Democracy* (Philadelphia: University of Pennsylvania Press, 2010), Chapter 2.
39 Chaloka Beyani, "Report of the Special Rapporteur on the Human Rights of Internally Displaced Persons on His Mission to Honduras," A/HRC/32/35/Add.4 (Geneva: United Nations Human Rights Council, 2016), 19.
40 Dirección de Atención a Víctimas, "Caracterización de la movilidad interna a causa de la violencia en El Salvador: informe final" (San Salvador: Ministerio de Justicia y Seguridad Pública, 2018).
41 Internal Displacement Monitoring Centre, "Global Overview 2015: People Internally Displaced by Conflict and Violence" (Geneva: Norwegian Refugee Council, 2015), 83.

42 Instituto Universitario de Opinión Pública, "Evaluación del país a fi-nales de 2014," Serie de informes 137 (Antiguo Cuscatlán: Universidad Centroamericana José Simeón Cañas, 2015), 42.

43 Dirección de Atención a Víctimas, "Caracterización de la movilidad interna a causa de la violencia en El Salvador."

44 Jonathan T. Hiskey et al., "Leaving the Devil You Know: Crime Victimization, US Deterrence Policy, and the Emigration Decision in Central America," *Latin American Research Review* 53, no. 3 (2018): 437, https://doi.org/10.25222/larr.147

45 Cantor, "As Deadly as Armed Conflict?"; Rodríguez Serna, "Fleeing Cartels and *Maras.*"

46 José Miguel Cruz, "Government Responses and the Dark Side of Gang Suppression in Central America," in *Maras: Gang Violence and Security in Central America*, ed. Thomas C. Bruneau, Lucía Dammert, and Elizabeth Skinner (Austin: University of Texas Press, 2011), 137–57.

47 Bob Fredericks, "Trump Dredges up 'Mexican Rapists' Comment in Latest Rant," *New York Post*, April 5, 2018, https://nypost.com/2018/04/05/trump-dredges-up-mexican-rapists-comment-in-latest-rant/

48 Gregory Korte and Alan Gomez, "Trump Ramps up Rhetoric on Undocumented Immigrants: 'These Aren't People. These Are Animals,'" *USA Today*, May 16, 2018, www.usatoday.com/story/news/politics/2018/05/16/trump-immigrants-animals-mexico-democrats-sanctuary-cities/617252002/

49 Julie Hirschfeld Davis and Katie Rogers, "Skirting Scandal, President Stokes Fear to Stay on Message for Midterms," *New York Times*, August 21, 2018.

50 Óscar Martínez et al., "Government Negotiates Reduction in Homicides with Gangs," *El Faro*, March 14, 2012, www.elfaro.net/es/201203/noticias/8061/

51 Sílvia Roque, "Between New Terrains and Old Dichotomies: Peacebuilding and the Gangs' Truce in El Salvador," *Contexto Internacional* 39, no. 3 (2017): 499–520, https://doi.org/10.1590/s0102-8529.2017390300003; Teresa Whitfield, "Mediating Criminal Violence: Lessons from the Gang Truce in El Salvador," Oslo Forum Papers (Geneva: Centre for Humanitarian Dialogue, 2013).

52 Ana Glenda Tager Rosado, "Parte del problema, parte de la solución: actores ilegales y reducción de violencia en El Salvador," in *Vulnerabilidad y violencia en América Latina y el Caribe*, ed. Markus Gottsbacher and John de Boer (City of Mexico: Siglo XXI Editores, 2016), 396.

53 José Miguel Cruz and Angélica Durán-Martínez, "Hiding Violence to Deal with the State: Criminal Pacts in El Salvador and Medellin," *Journal of Peace Research* 53, no. 2 (2016): 197–210, https://doi.org/10.1177/0022343315626239; Chris van der Borgh and Wim Savenije, "De-Securitising and Re-Securitising Gang Policies: The Funes Government and Gangs in El Salvador," *Journal of Latin American Studies* 47, no. 1 (2015): 149–76, doi:10.1017/S0022216X14000741

54 Charles M. Katz and Luis Enrique Amaya, "The Gang Truce as a Form of Violence Intervention" (San Salvador: Fundación Nacional para el Desarrollo, 2015), 39.

55 José Miguel Cruz and Angélica Durán-Martínez, "Hiding Violence to Deal with the State"; Chris van der Borgh and Wim Savenije, "The

Politics of Violence Reduction: Making and Unmaking the Salvadoran Gang Truce," *Journal of Latin American Studies*, forthcoming 2019.

56 Roberto Valencia and Carlos Martínez, "Hoy toca que los sedientos de sangre, los de las pandillas y los del gobierno, se sacien," *El Faro*, October 12, 2015, www.salanegra.elfaro.net/es/201510/entrevistas/17432/

57 van der Borgh and Savenije, "De-Securitising and Re-Securitising Gang Policies," 174.

58 José Raúl Hernández Maldonado and Saúl Enrique Mancía, "Análisis de contenido cualitativo: la construcción del concepto 'tregua entre pandillas' en las informaciones periodísticas de la sección 'Nación' de La Prensa Gráfica" (Thesis for Licenciate Degree in Journalism, Universidad de El Salvador, 2014), http://ri.ues.edu.sv/6401/1/; Erika M. Saca-Schader, "Coverage of the Gang Peace Process in El Salvador by the *El Diario de Hoy*: Framing and Diffusion of Innovations Theory" (Thesis for Master of Arts in Communications, California State University, 2015); Olga Vásquez Monzón and Amparo Marroquín Parducci, "Entre gritos y silencios: la narrativa de la prensa salvadoreña sobre la tregua entre pandillas," *Nueva Sociedad* 249 (2014): 86–96.

59 Zeid Ra'ad Al Hussein, "Statement by UN High Commissioner for Human Rights Zeid Ra'ad Al Hussein at the End of His Mission to El Salvador," Office of the United Nations High Commissioner for Human Rights, November 17, 2017, www.ohchr.org/EN/NewsEvents/Pages/DisplayNews.aspx?NewsID=22412&LangID=E

60 Agnes Callamard, "Report of the Special Rapporteur on Extrajudicial, Summary or Arbitrary Executions on Her Mission to El Salvador," *A/HRC/38/44/Add.2* (Geneva: United Nations Human Rights Council, June 18, 2018), para. 15.

61 Asamblea Legislativa, "Disposiciones especiales para el control y seguimiento de la población retornada salvadoreña calificada como miembros de maras, pandillas o agrupaciones ilícitas," *Diario Oficial* 416, no. 125 (July 6, 2017): 9–16.

62 General Assembly, *Universal Declaration of Human Rights* (Paris: United Nations, 1948).

3 The Photograph Seen "Around the World"

The Media, the Migrant Mother from Honduras, and the U.S.-Backed Military Coup of 2009

Robin Andersen

At the Border

On Sunday, November 25, 2018, a *Reuters'* photojournalist who had been travelling for over two weeks with a large group of Central American migrants heading for the U.S. border at San Ysidro, California, captured a picture that would dramatically change the news discourse through which the "caravan" of "invaders" had been framed for weeks. The photograph travelled over the digital technologies of social media, and appeared on the front pages of major news outlets. Writers for the *Washington Post* and the *New York Times* discussed the power of the picture itself, and it was quickly used as irrefutable evidence of a policy gone terribly wrong.[1] The image provided a visual critique of U.S. immigration and border policies enacted by the Trump Administration, and led to tie-in stories that were also critical of those policies.

The "Migrant Mother"

The image shows a Honduran woman running across a desolate landscape transected by a dirty line of water that was once a stream. The scene is framed by two border walls that run three-quarters of the way across the top of the image. One is chain-link, topped with razor-wire, the other a solid structure that dominates the space below it. The woman featured in the foreground grasps the tiny arms of her two young girls wearing diapers, who stumble on their slim bare legs running at either side of their mother. One is barefoot. Flip flops cling to the feet of the child on the right. At the lower third of the image, a bloom of smoke grows larger as it rises closer to them on the right. They are running from tear gas that has been lobbed across the border at the unarmed migrants attempting to scale the border wall and reach the United States. Holding her tongue at the side of her mouth, the mother's face is a complex mix of fear, determination, struggle, and power as she looks down at one of the girls. She grasps the small arms, almost dragging the toddlers away from the smoke and out of harm's way. The terrible irony of the picture resides in the bright, multicolored tee-shirt the woman wears, as the large blue eyes of the blond animated character from the Disney movie *Frozen* look out from the woman's body, bearing witnessing to the scene. The blue eyes now appear to be alarmed. The incongruous tee-shirt covers the woman's torso, and the very short sleeves reveal her strong, full brown arms, a surprising contrast to the way the shirt might look on a youthful Disney fan at the mall.

The image exposed, in so many ways, the false language of demonization that had characterized the Central Americans migrants for weeks—as criminals, terrorists, and impostors on their way to invade the United States. It revealed the simple truth that the migrants are just like us. They are recognizable; mothers and children in diapers with the same sensibilities and aspirations that we hold, struggling to be embraced by a country they admire, even donning the tie-products of American popular culture. Though unarmed, they are nevertheless under attack by the most powerful military on the globe, and maligned in ways that the picture seems to expose, as obviously false.

The following day, *Reuters* published an article quoting a statement by Vicki Gass, a Senior Policy Advisor for Central America at the NGO, Oxfam America saying, "Images of barefoot children choking on tear gas thrown by U.S. Customs and Border Patrol should shock us to our core."[2] Indeed, the press did seem to be shaken to its core by the visual documentation at the border. The tone and content of media coverage dramatically changed. The picture had precipitated a classic break in the news frame, a phenomenon noted historically as *cognitive dissonance*, when suddenly the standard media tropes no longer seem adequate to the task of explaining or justifying government policies. The security discourses of the "invasion" frame no longer seemed relevant to describe or understand the people arriving in great numbers at the U.S. border.

Much of the coverage in the weeks leading up to the arrival of the caravan at the border had been framed around a militarized Trumpian discourse that understood the forced migration of refugees underway through Mexico as a deliberate, orchestrated invasion of criminals. As the refugee caravan grew closer, numerous stories detailed the logistics of the U.S. military amassing to head them off, complete with the articulation by military officials justifying such troop movements. But the running woman holding fast to her two toddlers soon became the iconic symbol that belied Trump's false claims.

As the news cycle progressed throughout the week that followed, coverage in the mainstream media, excluding Fox News Network, became almost singularly critical, and included a variety of voices from democrats to professors who detailed in earnest, opposition to Administration policies. With Trump at the helm on his Twitter feed, the Administration fought back with a barrage of more false claims that added fodder for the critical media frame taking hold in the press. For example, by Tuesday the *Washington Post* carried a lengthy article about how the *Reuters'* photographer captured the image of the migrant mother.[3] Embedded within the report, another headline printed in blue, carries a link to a different story titled "Why tear gas, lobbed at migrants on the southern border is banned in warfare."[4] This article by Alex Horton explains that CS gas is a strong chemical with many painful, even deadly side effects including nausea, vomiting, gaging, and sometimes asphyxiation. One infant exposed to CS gas developed "severe pneumonitis" requiring a month of hospitalization. The author goes on to cite an expert who warns, "the effects of tear gas on younger bodies is not well documented."[5] He then includes a statement by Democratic governor-elect of California, Gavin Newsom who tweeted:

These children are barefoot. In diapers. Choking on tear gas. Women and children who left their lives behind—seeking peace and asylum—were met with violence and fear. That's not my America. We're a land of refuge. Of hope. Of freedom. And we will not stand for this.[6]

The same day the *Huffington Post* noted that wire-service journalists on the scene had "witnessed children screaming and coughing amid the gas."[7] Another startling headline embedded into the *Washington Post* story read, "You could actually put it on your nachos and eat it, Fox guest says of gas used at the Mexican border."[8] This article refers to an interview with Ron Colburn, the president of the Border Patrol Foundation, who tells Fox News that "it's literally water, pepper, with a small amount of alcohol for evaporation purposes. It's natural, you could actually put it on your nachos and eat it."[9] The *Washington Post* writer carefully cites Sven-Eric Jordt, an associate professor at Duke University School of Medicine, explaining that pepper spray and CS gas are quite different, and that the toxic chemical capsaicin used in tear gas is "several thousand-fold higher" in concentrations and "would never be used" on food.[10] Links to other related, and equally critical stories are included at the end of these articles.

Many news outlets were often satirically critical of the "nacho tear gas" story, and others countered Trump's increasingly exaggerated declarations that were easily discounted. One headline announced, "Trump Falsely Claims Border Agents Were Badly Hurt In Migrant Tear Gas Clashes: He said the tear gas was 'very safe' as he slammed the migrants as violent criminals."[11] The article goes on to say that the President claimed that three U.S. Customs and Border Patrol agents "were very badly hurt, getting hit with rocks and stones" after closing the San Ysidro port of entry on Sunday. Reporters had only to cite officials at the border to refute assertions that border officials had been hurt. As one reporter states, "This contradicts" official statements by CBP commissioner Kevin McAleenan who "denied that any border agents were injured in the scuffle."[12]

An insightful comment made about the Central American migrants came from an unlikely media source. On the show *The Five* (11/26/18), Geraldo Rivera said, "I want to say I am ashamed." Making an apt analogy to violence entertainment culture and the logic of demonization, Rivera said, "We treat these people... as if they're zombies from *The Walking Dead*. We arrested 42 people; eight of them were women with children." In the words that followed, Rivera opens the topic to include the context of past U.S. military involvement in Central America. Rivera somewhat clumsily but directly makes the point that migrants "are a part of our continent. We can pay attention to our neighbors, for goodness' sake, and ... **how have we destabilized these governments over the decades**." [emphasis added] The point is spoken and then quickly disappears, but not without being noticed by the *Washington Post*'s Alex Horton who observed that after the statement Rivera's co-host cut him off. Horton writes, "Rivera had apparently opened the aperture too far."[13] Even as Horton admits that comments about past U.S. military interventions are subjects ignored by media, he too drops the point, making no further comment on the topic.

The photograph of the Honduran woman that came to be known as the Migrant Mother is a reference to the famous photograph taken by Dorothea Lange in 1936 in Nipomo California, while working for the U.S. Farm Security Administration (FSA).[14] Like the image snapped in 2019, Lange's image is understood to bear powerful witness to the plight of migrants. Lange's Mother was an internally displaced person from the Great Depression, and the picture altered historical perceptions at the time. Like Lange's image, the photograph taken of the Honduran mother was powerful, and it led to media critical of border militarization.

But mainstream media missed the opportunity to offer the broader context and the conditions in the country the migrant mother was forced to leave—Honduras. Though reporting challenged such weaponized logics as the use of tear-gas and cited the rules of war, even offering an inchoate humanitarian narrative, it failed to present a counter narrative, one that would explain the active role played by the United States in destabilizing Honduras. Only a few alternative media outlets offered information about conditions in Honduras able to explain why migrants have been forced to leave their country. Following the same historical pattern of military interventions in the hemisphere, in the twenty-first century the United States has helped dismantle democratic institutions in Honduras, which have led to a failed economy, violations of human rights and increasing violence. I will now turn to that history, and how it has been narrated in U.S. media.

The 2009 Coup d'état in Honduras and the Forced Migration of Refugees

Honduras is a country rich in resources, yet one of the most unequal, and the second-poorest in the Americas. Most of the country's wealth is owned and controlled by a small elite.[15] On the night of June 28, 2009, a coup d'état deposed the country's democratically elected president, Manuel Zelaya. Still in his pajamas, the president, surrounded by rifle-carrying military men, was forced onto a plane and taken to Costa Rica. Though Zelaya came from a family made wealthy by the logging and timber industry, and was elected in 2006 on a conservative platform, within a year he had begun to lead the country toward modest economic and social reforms. Those reforms angered the Honduran military, multinational corporate interests, and the country's wealthy elite.

In *A History of Honduras*, Thomas Leonard notes that Zelaya's government introduced free education for all children in Honduras and provided school meals for more than one and a half million poor students.[16] In addition, the minimum wage rose by an estimated 80 percent and domestic employees were integrated into the social security system. His government began to subsidize small farmers, and the interest rates banks were allowed to charge against personal loans were reduced, making it easier for the country's poor to borrow money.[17] In addition, the state provided direct aid to help 200,000 families in extreme poverty. Writing in *The New Statesman* less than three months after her father was deposed, Xiomara Zelaya explains that implementing the social programs threatened the interests of global capital. Cutting fuel prices "caused direct confrontations with the major oil multinationals." She continued,

> He denounced the plundering of the state electricity and telecommunications enterprises, which had been forced into bankruptcy. He worked for their recovery and to avoid privatizing the few remaining state firms in a country where some 80 per cent of our resources have been privatized.[18]

Overall, Xiomara notes that the poverty rate was reduced by almost 10 percent over the course of his presidency. Because of these policies, her father had become a target. Significantly, Zelaya had pledged to resolve longstanding land conflicts between peasant farmers and agribusinesses, a point we will return to below.

The United Sates, Hillary Clinton, and the Military Coup

Governments across Latin America condemned Zelaya's kidnapping as a "military coup," and Honduras was suspended by the Organization of American States. The United Nations, the European Union (EU), and President Barack Obama immediately called for the President's restoration, but as Secretary of State, Hillary Clinton supported the coup.[19] Speaking to the *New York Daily News* in early 2016, then presidential candidate Clinton justified her position saying that the military had not violated Honduran law. "Now I didn't like the way it looked or the way they did it, but they had a strong argument that they had followed the constitution and the legal precedents."[20] Yet in a diplomatic cable released by WikiLeaks, the U.S. Ambassador to Honduras in Tegucigalpa at the time, Hugo Llorens, agreed that the coup violated Honduran constitutional law. He wrote, "There is no doubt that the military, Supreme Court and National Congress conspired on June 28 in what constituted an illegal and unconstitutional coup against the executive branch."[21] In addition, Clinton's director of policy planning Anne-Marie Slaughter emailed her on August 16, 2009, urging Secretary Clinton to "find that (the) coup was a 'military coup' under U.S. law." Slaughter warned, "we are losing ground in Latin America every day the Honduras crisis continues." She went on to say, "Even our friends are beginning to think we are not really committed to the norm of constitutional democracy."[22]

There had been no doubt of Hillary Clinton's role in backing the coup since 2014 with the publication of her memoir *Hard Choices.* She wrote,

> In the subsequent days I spoke with my counterparts around the hemisphere ... We strategized on a plan to restore order in Honduras and ensure that free and fair elections could be held quickly and legitimately, which would render the question of Zelaya moot.[23]

Clinton's strategy to press for elections without restoring the President left the United States politically isolated in the hemisphere. The "Rio Group," an organization that included every Latin American and Caribbean government, demanded "that Zelaya's restoration be a precondition for recognizing elections."[24] But the United States continued to push for elections, which were held in November 2009. International election observers, as well as many Honduran candidates, boycotted the process, but "the U.S. bucked the trend, funding its own observers and then recognizing the results, thereby souring relations with the hemisphere."[25] The post-coup violence against Zelaya's supporters guaranteed that less than half of the electorate voted. "'Meanwhile, the crackdown was brutal,' said Karen Spring of the Honduras Solidarity Network. 'People were beaten, tortured, disappeared, jailed illegally. There were no conditions for free and fair elections; there was no peaceful transition.'"[26]

A conservative politician Porfirio Lobos, (whose family members remain intimately connected to the drug trade) became the new president. As Dana Frank observed, these were old-fashioned "demonstration elections."[27]

Indeed, it shored up a military coup in one of the poorest countries in Central America, yet the one with the closet ties to the U.S. militarily. As it turns out, the U.S. military was working furiously behind the scenes to block Zelaya's return.

Military Ties That Bind

In late 2017, details of how the coup and its aftermath unfolded came to light through investigations published by *The Intercept* and the Center for Economic and Policy Research.[28] Drawing on unpublished government records and dozens of interviews with high-ranking U.S. and Honduran military officials and policy-makers, and pouring over email communications and other documents obtained through FOIA requests, researcher Jake Johnston offers a glimpse into what happened. Behind the scenes, the U.S. military lobbied Congress and the Obama Administration to let the new regime stand, and Republican law makers were courted in Washington by Honduran elites who felt threatened by Zelaya's economic and political reforms. But ultimately, it was the State Department under Hillary Clinton that followed the U.S. military's direction. Most importantly, the documentation reveals the powerful and enduring connections between the Honduran military and the Center for Hemispheric Defense Studies (CHDS), housed at the National Defense University in Washington, D.C.[29] Hundreds of Hondurans have been trained at the CHDS over the years, and the close ties between U.S. and Honduran military personnel remains today. Honduras is home to the largest U.S. military base in the hemisphere and is key to U.S. geopolitical strategy in the region.

Johnston provides a detailed timeline of how the coup took place.

> In fact, the two militaries were so close that, American military officers and diplomats were at a party the night before the coup at the U.S. defense attaché's house with their Honduran counterparts. At 9 p.m., while at the party, Col. Kenneth Rodriguez, the U.S. Military Group commander in Honduras, received an urgent call asking him to meet with the head of the Honduran military, Gen. Romeo Vásquez Velásquez.

The Military Group operates outside the embassy's chain of command, and coordinates training programs and security protocols with CHDS. Over the course of the following weeks Johnston has pieced together the details of how the coup prevailed in Honduras.

According to email records obtained by Johnston through FOIA requests, after the coup, staff at CHDS were in regular communication with staff at the Pentagon's Latin American subsidiary, the U.S. Southern Command, known as SOUTHCOM. Kenneth

LaPlante, the deputy director of CHDS at the time of the coup, explained to Johnston that the United States wouldn't want to push Zelaya back into office and so it would give the coup government some time to set things up before moving on to elections.

The United States simply had too much to lose to take any other position. Most importantly among them was the geostrategic use of Soto Cano, the military base 50 miles outside of the Honduran capital, Tegucigalpa. In the early 1980s, the base was established as a staging ground for U.S support for Central American military regimes and right-wing insurgencies, most notably the Contras in neighboring Nicaragua. When SOUTHCOM's mission pivoted from fighting communism to the War on Drugs, Soto Cano became more strategic as other bases closed. "In the 1990s, SOUTHCOM's budget increased more than any other U.S. military regional command." While in office President Zelaya had spoken of using the base as a commercial airport. In June 2008, as Johnston writes, "in response to Zelaya's plans, then-U.S. Ambassador Charles Ford wrote that the U.S. would keep a 'low public profile' while working to 'protect U.S. security interests at Soto Cano.'"[30] Ford took a job with SOUTHCOM after leaving his embassy post in Honduras.

Hillary Clinton would adopt the talking points written by military commanders to carry out sham elections, in direct contradiction to President Obama's official statement to restore Zelaya's Presidency. As Johnston puts it, "Hidden actors during the crisis tilted Honduras toward chaos, undermined official U.S. policy after the coup, and ushered in a new era of militarization that has left a trail of violence and repression in its wake."[31]

Violent Repression After the Coup

Political violence in Honduras increased dramatically after the coup. President Zelaya had listened to the voices of protest from native Hondurans, and acted to block a series of hydroelectric dam projects in environmentally sensitive areas.[32] Less than a year after Zelaya was ousted, the new rightwing government had begun to license hundreds of mega-projects, including mines and hydroelectric dams, many on native lands. Scholar Daniel Beckman at the Council on Hemispheric Affairs noted that the Honduran coup "represented a full takeover by the country's big ranching, trafficking, oil-palm, and mining interests."[33]

Environmental campaigners became the targets of corporate backed military and para-military repression. According to data compiled by the Committee of Relatives of the Disappeared/Detained (COFADEH), the leading Honduran human rights organization, by early 2012, state security forces had assassinated more than 300 people,[34] and 34 members of the opposition had disappeared or been killed.[35] In 2012, 20 people were killed daily, and *Reuters* reported that it had the highest murder rate of any country.[36] The coup sent the country back to the brutality of the Cold War that characterized the U.S. driven military policies of the 1980s, as we detailed in Chapter 1. Advocate and activists Bertha Oliva, founder of COFADEH, had witnessed her husband get dragged away in the night to be murdered in 1981. In an interview with Yolanda Polo published in 2013, Oliva observed that the post-coup regimes were "unimaginably worse than the death-squad-ridden military-run regimes that prevailed in the 1980s."[37] Decades of hard-won democratization and strengthening of civil society in Honduras have been permanently reversed by the coup.

From the beginning, drug traffickers were deeply embedded within the post-coup government, and the police force had close ties to the drug trade. By 2013, 70 percent of the police would be found "beyond saving," paid off or themselves engaged in organized crime, "including trafficking, extortion, rape, and murder for hire. In addition, 12 percent of the members of Congress were narco-traffickers."[38]

Though the political assassinations and government corruption emboldened violence from gangs and drug traffickers, U.S. media coverage frequently misses the political nature of the killings, and the government's role in the drug trade. As Honduras became one of the world's most dangerous countries for environmental defenders,[39] U.S. media frequently attributed the violence singularly to drug cartels. Emblematic of such coverage is a *TIME* magazine report from 2014 that states, "Due to the influx of Mexican drug cartels that funnel U.S.-bound drugs through the country violence has been on the rise in recent years."[40] But drugs violence is a more recent symptom of the dismantling of Honduran democracy at the hands of right-wing governments since the coup. A point we will return to below.

Lawyers, journalists, women, and the LGBT community were hit hard, as the murder rates for targeted groups escalated in post-coup Honduras. *TeleSUR* reported that over 100 lawyers were killed in the first five years after the coup.[41] By 2016, "229 LGBT people had been murdered—an average of 30 every year, according to the NGO Cattrachas."[42] Dana Frank observed that murders of Honduran women became so widespread that it must be considered *femicide*.[43] The Committee to Protect Journalists reported that 13 journalists had been killed, stating, "Honduran press continued to suffer the violent fallout of the 2009 coup." They documented the killing of four broadcast journalists in 2011 and stated, "A climate of violence and widespread impunity has made the country one of the most dangerous in the region."[44]

Contextualizing the nature of the killings, which are on the increase in the hemisphere, in April 2015, *Global Witness* published a report titled "How Many More?" showing that the killings of environmental activists are increasing in Central and South America, "with indigenous communities hardest hit."[45] Killings in Honduras top the list. The report states, "Some are shot by police during protests, others gunned down by hired assassins. As companies go in search of new land to exploit, increasingly people are paying the ultimate price for standing in their way." Most people are dying "amid disputes over hydropower, mining and agri-business." Many of the murders are hard to document because they are carried out in remote villages or deep within the jungle, "where communities lack access to communications and the media. It's likely many more killings are escaping public records." The lack of reporting seemed to embolden state repression.

This is not to say that U.S. media were totally silent on developments in Honduras, especially up to 2016. Reports citing compelling documentation were included through the online news outlets of alternative media, such as *TruthOut, Common Dreams, The Nation, The National Catholic Reporter, The Intercept, Democracy Now!,* and even the *New York Daily News* when Hillary Clinton became a presidential candidate in 2016. *The Guardian* newspaper in the U.K. frequently published hard-hitting stories on developments in Honduras. Such press reports relied on the research and documentation of human rights organizations, legal advocacy groups, activists, and scholarly research. Many fewer meaningful press reports were published in U.S. mainstream media.

In March 2016, Honduras came under the unwanted glare of a global media spotlight with the extrajudicial assassination of a prominent international environmental leader named Berta Cáceres. Born in 1971 in La Esperanza, Honduras, Cáceres was an intelligent political critic, social activist, and opposition leader who fought tirelessly on behalf of the indigenous Lenca community in her country. She led a global campaign against the Agua Zarca hydroelectric dam, and won the prestigious Goldman Environmental Prize in 2015.[46] One month after her murder, *The Guardian* published an extensive report by a military whistle blower using the pseudonym Cruz, who had seen names and photographs on a hit list held by his superior. The soldier had seen Cáceres's name on the list given to a military police unit. In the summer of 2015, the police unit, the Inter-institutional Security Force (Fusina), had received training from 300 U.S. marines and F.B.I. agents. In the months leading up to her murder, Cáceres had reported 33 death threats linked to the campaign and told international human rights staffers that her name was on a "hit list."[47]

Cruz told *The Guardian* that he recognized other faces as leaders from the Bajo Aguán region—where another military task-force, the Xatruch, is based. The area had been the setting for a series of violent land disputes between powerful palm oil magnates and local farmers. As *The Guardian* notes, "More than 100 people, mainly peasant activists, have been killed, many at the hands of state or private security forces."[48] Also on the hit list were two high-profile members of the United Peasant Movement (Muca) Johnny Rivas and Vitalino Álvarez, along with 123 other activists from Bajo Aguán, where a long-simmering land conflict pitted powerful agro-industrial elites against impoverished small farmers.[49] In 2014, the Inter-American Commission on Human Rights (IACHR) identified the activists as "requiring urgent protective measures," to prevent them from also being assassinated.[50] Berta Cáceres's older sister Flores told *The Guardian* that much of the violence in Honduras could be traced directly back "to a sell-off of mining and hydroelectric concessions that followed the coup. 'These concessions generated violence which eventually killed Berta. We're still paying the consequences of the coup,' she said."[51]

Berta Cáceres family has fought hard to bring her murderers to justice in the nearly dismantled judicial system in Honduras.[52] Though a trail convicted those that carried out the murder of Berta Cáceres, the corporate heads that called for her killing were excluded from prosecution.[53] Victor Fernandez, a prominent human rights attorney and lawyer representing the Cáceres family, insisted that her assassination was carried out by either the Honduran government or by "the paramilitary structure of companies." Fernandez went on to say, "Honduras is the victim of international theft" because of its rich national resources, referring to the minerals, rivers, and forests in the country. "Cáceres was killed because she was confronting the extractive model."[54]

The Migrants

In Honduras, these words from TV reporter, Olin Castro, in San Pedro Sula were published in *TIME* magazine at the end of October 2018, "This is the worst moment ever for my country."[55] Unlike other migrations that have left from Mexico, the 2018 caravan started in Honduras itself, organized by activist on social media. It gained momentum and numbers from TV reports that caught the attention of Hondurans who were at a "breaking point." In a long piece, mostly about their hardships along the journey—and quotes from Trump, followed by the words of migrants responding to the President—the article takes two paragraphs to explain their reasons for leaving. It states that Honduras has suffered "chronically high levels of violence for several years as street gangs and drug cartels fight for territory." The report includes stories of individuals under attack, whose family member have been brutally murdered. A 20-year-old named Nelson Uribe told *TIME*, "I was hiding in my house, terrified to go out. The caravan gave me a chance to leave."[56]

Economic reasons are also given, with a witness testimonial who cited poverty and hunger, "especially following recent price hikes. 'We just can't afford to live. It was a question of leaving or slowly starving to death,' said Orisa Fernandez, 40."[57] These are compelling narratives, but they tell only a fraction of the story. They fail to include the reasons for the economic decline in Honduras, and how corruption and exploitation have pushed the country into brutality and violence.

In her book, *The Long Honduran Night*, Professor Dana Frank explains the emergence of gangs in recent years in Honduras, and makes the connections between the coup, government corruption, and out migration.[58] Such connections are rarely made in mainstream press reports, a point that Frank also notes.

The Post-Coup Economic Regime: Corruption, Gang Violence, and Migration

A report published in May 2017 by the *Carnegie Endowment for International Peace*, specifically links migration to corruption and to U.S. support for the Honduran regime. "Urban violence and out migration are byproducts of the corruption of the very government that enjoys U.S. and European Union support to combat those ills."[59] In blunt language, author Sarah Chayes, describes

Honduras as a "kleptocracy," and summarizes government corruption in its broad parameters: "corruption is the operating system of sophisticated networks that link together public and private sectors and out-and-out criminals including killers."[60]

Five years after the coup, gangs were fully embedded within Honduran society. As Frank has written, gangs were the consequence of the coup regime's ongoing destruction of the rule of law. By 2014, the full effects of that destruction were manifest. Police were deeply embedded in illegal activities. "Drug traffickers took over a broad swath of the daily life in Honduras in part because the elites who ran the government permitted and even profited from it. Who was the gang, in this story?"[61] As gangs spread, they expanded into a variety of income-generating activities, especially including the extortion of small businesses and transportation operators. "Working hand-in-glove with local police who took their own cut of the proceeds, gang extortionists were operating throughout the big cities by 2014."[62] For that year alone, extortionists cost Hondurans an estimated $2 million. Small-business owners were especially hard hit by gang shakedowns, and as the amount of payoffs increased, so did the violence associated with the failure to pay.

Retributive violence of this sort was only possible because the judiciary had been dismantled, and was largely corrupt, and the criminal justice system "functioned to protect the crooked and the murderous."[63] Without a functioning criminal justice system, human rights violations escalated. The U.S. State Department itself called attention to the week justice system, and the widespread impunity for attacks against the civilian population.[64] In a 2014 report on Honduras, Human Rights Watch documented how perpetrators of killings and other violent crimes were rarely brought to justice.[65]

Media Coverage of Honduran Poverty

As we have seen above, when reasons for migration are offered in press reports, journalists include interviews with refugees who say they left their country for economic reasons, citing fear of starvation, or simply a "better life." But again, reporting ends there, without explanation of why the country is so poor, especially one so rich in natural resources. Virtually no mainstream press accounts covering the migrant caravan acknowledge that under President Zalaya, the poor benefitted enormously. Zelaya's Presidency improved conditions for the lowest income sectors, even allowing some to enter the middle class. In place of explanation, the economy, like the violence, has no origins. It is simply the country itself. The people are violent and poor, and Honduras itself is "othered," a place and a country that just doesn't work. As Frank states, it is as if the Honduran economy "were just a natural disaster, not the product of five years of deliberate economic policies."[66] She goes on to explain, "Pre-coup Honduras had never been a golden age, economically. But the country did have a functioning state that had provided basic services to large numbers of Hondurans." Honduran economy was based on agriculture, manufacturing enterprises that served a regional and sometimes broader market, and services. Many people were seriously poor. "But there were measures, and hopes, and thriving small businesses, and a middle class."[67] After President Zelaya was illegally kidnapped in the military coup, and Roberto Micheletti was positioned as the new president (and Hillary Clinton and the U.S. military waited for "free and fair" elections), one of the first things Micheletti and the coup's perpetrators did was to rob "the country's coffers blind.[68] They drained the teacher's pension fund, and thereafter the elites stole broadly from the Honduras state in rampaging corruption.

Over the past decade, the U.S.-back post-coup regime has destroyed much of the functioning state and modest economy that once existed in Honduras. The country has been transformed into a violent, failed state whose citizens are systematically brutalized and unable to make a living. The wealthy elite continue to thrive, as they are tied to the multinational extractive industries and protected by paramilitary security forces who assassinate in increasing numbers, the brave environmental defenders who hold tight to their land and communities. The corrupt government and brutal security forces are funded by the United States under the guise of fighting gangs and the war on drugs, and the police and military take part in the killings and profit from drug trafficking at the expense of the people they are supposed to protect. This is the context that has caused the forced migration of Hondurans and set them on a journey north, where they arrive at the borders of the very country that has caused their suffering, a country in deep denial of its responsibility to the refugees it has created. Worse, instead of itself obeying its own long-standing rule of law, that refugees who cross the border are entitled to apply for asylum, the United States ignores international human rights protocols and blames and demonizes the migrants, claiming they are the criminals, and arresting them. This is the narrative that stays hidden under security discourses that justify the criminalization of Honduran refugees.

Conclusion

Though President Barack Obama made public statements condemning the coup, behind the scenes, over the course of several months, Secretary of State Hillary Clinton recognized the coup as legitimate, ignored the escalating repression against the people of Honduras, and called for new elections, all actions that have allowed Honduras to descend into the violent chaotic country recognizable today. Though the brutal, untenable conditions in Honduras are tied to the migrations of Honduran refugees seeking asylum in the United States, the role the United States played in backing the coup is hushed and silenced, and omitted in most mainstream media coverage.

The woman caught through the camera lens of the *Reuters'* photographer, the one running from tear gas, holding tight to the small arms of her two young girls, had come from Honduras seeking asylum in the United States. Though the press and most Americans recoiled from the brutal irony of the image, and the photograph shook the language of "invasion" that had dominated the press for weeks, the image itself could not tell the history of violence and the story of U.S. involvement in dismantling the rule of law in Honduras. For a short time, it changed the language of invasion to a different set of discourses based on humanitarian principles. NGOs found a momentary voice, and politicians critical of such treatment evoked the moral conscience of the country. But images and coverage did not spark a broad public discussion of the causes of the violence that has sent the refugees on their forced migrations northward. And it did not lead to a historical perspective able to illuminate the role of U.S. militarism in destabilizing the countries of the Norther Triangle. Only when this history is foregrounded and the interconnections made, will a meaningful policy discussion about Central American migration take place.

On December 8, 2018, a 7-year-old Guatemalan girl named Jakelin died in the custody of Customs and Border Protection agents. Though her death led to more scrutiny and criticism of Border Patrol practices, as we will see in the next chapter, like reporting about Honduran migrants, news reporting of Jakelin's death offered almost no information about the U.S. role in destabilizing Guatemala. We will now turn to that country and find that similar internal economic patterns and U.S. military involvement have led to out-migration from Guatemala as well.

Notes

1 Kristine Phillips, "How a Photographer Captured the Image of a Migrant Mother and her Children Fleeing Tear Gas," *Washington Post*, November 27, 2018, www.washingtonpost.com/world/2018/11/26/how-photographer-captured-image-migrant-mother-her-children-fleeing-tear-gas/?utm_term=.627706b8791a

2 Susan Heavey and Lizbeth Diaz, "Mexico Call for Full Investigation of US Tear Gas at Border," *Reuters*, November 26, 2018, www.reuters.com/article/us-usa-immigration-idUSKCN1NV1MU

3 Ibid., Kristine Phillips, 2018.

4 Alex Horton, "Why Tear Gas Lobbed at Migrants on the Southern Border is Banned in Warfare," *Washington Post*, November 27, 2018, www.washingtonpost.com/national-security/2018/11/26/why-tear-gas-lobbed-migrants-southern-border-is-banned-warfare/?utm_term=.aa246d31ccd4

5 Ibid., Alex Horton, 2018.

6 Ibid., Alex Horton, 2018.

7 Willa Frej, "Trump Falsely Claims Border Agents Were Badly Hurt in Migrant Tear Gas Clashes," *Huffington Post*, November 27, 2018, www.huffingtonpost.com/entry/trump-defended-tear-gas-migrants_us_5bfd17aee4b0771fb6bdbd78

8 Michael Brice-Saddler, "You Could Actually Put it on You Nachos and Eat it: Fox Guest Says of Gas Used at the Mexican Border," *Washington Post*, November 26, 2018, www.washingtonpost.com/politics/2018/11/26/you-could-actually-put-it-your-nachos-eat-it-fox-guest-says-gas-used-mexican-border/?utm_term=.5f3ee3f8307a

9 *Media Matters*, "*Fox & Friends* Guest Defends Use of Pepper Spray on Migrant Caravan: "It's Natural. You could Actually Put it on Your Nachos and Eat It," November 28, 2018, www.mediamatters.org/video/2018/11/26/fox-friends-guest-defends-use-pepper-spray-migrant-caravan-its-natural-you-could-actually-put-it/222140

10 Ibid., Michael Brice-Saddler, 2018.

11 Ibid., Willa Frej, 2018.

12 Ibid., Willa Frej, 2018.

13 Alex Horton, "Geraldo Rivera Urges Conservatives to Stop Treating Migrants as 'zombies from *The Walking Dead*,'" *Washington Post*, November 27, 2018, www.washingtonpost.com/politics/2018/11/27/geraldo-rivera-urges-conservatives-stop-treating-migrants-zombies-walking-dead/?utm_term=.8e70834456d7

14 MOMA Learning, "Migrant Mother, Nipomo, California," www.moma.org/learn/moma_learning/dorothea-lange-migrant-mother-nipomo-california-1936/

15 Nina Lakhani, "Did Hillary Clinton Stand by as Honduran Coup ushered in Era of Violence?" *The Guardian*, August 31, 2016, www.theguardian.com/world/2016/aug/31/hillary-clinton-honduras-violence-manuel-zelaya-berta-caceres

16 Thomas M. Leonard, *A History of Honduras*, ABC-CIO 2011.

17 Benjamin Dangl, "The Road to Zalaya's Return: Money, Guns and Social Movements in Honduras," *Upside Down World*, September 21, 2009,

http://upsidedownworld.org/archives/honduras/the-road-to-zelayas-return-money-guns-and-social-movements-in-honduras/
18 Xiomara Zelaya, "My Father has been Punished for Helping Honduras," *The New Statesman*, September 17, 2009, www.newstatesman.com/international-politics/2009/09/coup-regime-honduras-father
19 Ibid., Nina Lakhani, 2016.
20 Juan Gonzales, "Hillary Clinton's Policy was a Latin American Crimes Story," *New York Daily News*, April 12, 2016, www.nydaily news.com/news/national/gonzalez-clinton-policy-latin-american-crime-story-article-1.2598456
21 Ibid., Juan Gonzales, 2016.
22 Daniel Beckman, "A Labyrinth of Deception: Secretary Clinton and the Honduran Coup," Council on Hemispheric Affairs, April 12, 2017, www.coha.org/a-labyrinth-of-deception-secretary-clinton-and-the-honduran-coup/#_edn7
23 Hillary Clinton removed these words from the paperback edition of *Hard Choices*.
24 Jake Johnston, "How Pentagon Official May Have Encouraged a 2009 Coup in Honduras," *The Intercept*, August 29, 2017, https://theintercept.com/2017/08/29/honduras-coup-us-defense-departmetnt-center-hemispheric-defense-studies-chds/
25 Ibid., Jake Johnston, 2017.
26 Ibid., Nina Lakhani, 2016.
27 *Democracy Now*, "'It Is Not a Natural Disaster': Dana Frank on How U.S.-Backed Coup in Honduras Fueled Migrant Crisis," November 28, 2018, www.democracynow.org/2018/11/28/it_is_not_a_natural_disaster
28 Center for Economic and Policy Research, "Investigation Reveals New Details of 2009 Military Coup in Honduras," http://cepr.net/press-center/press-releases/investigation-reveals-new-details-of-us-role-in-2009-honduras-military-coup
29 Ibid., Jake Johnston, 2017.
30 Ibid., Jake Johnston, 2017.
31 Ibid., Jake Johnston, 2017.
32 Alex Emmons, "Death Squads are back in Honduras, Activists Tell Congress," *The Intercept*, April 2016, https://theintercept.com/2016/04/12/death-squads-are-back-in-honduras-honduran-activists-tell-congress/
33 Ibid., Daniel Beckman, 2017.
34 Dana Frank, "In Honduras, A Mess Helped by the U.S.," *New York Times*, January 27, 2012, www.nytimes.com/2012/01/27/opinion/in-honduras-a-mess-helped-by-the-us.html
35 The Committee of Relatives of the Disappeared in Honduras (COFA-DEH), in Spanish, Comité de Familiares de Detenidos Desaparecidos en Honduras. The organization was founded in 1982 to document the human rights abuses in Honduras as the United States instituted the NATIONAL SECURITY doctrine that included "a systematic and selective form of human rights violations. The most emblematic violations where torture, murders and enforced disappearances." www.cofadeh.org/html/historia/historia_ingles.htm

36 Maya Rhodan, "Honduras is Still the Murder Capital of the World," *TIME*, February 17, 2014, http://world.time.com/2014/02/17/honduras-is-still-the-murder-capital-of-the-world/

37 Cited in, Ibid., Daniel Beckman, 2017.

38 Ibid., Daniel Beckman, 2017.

39 Nina Lakhani, "Berta Cáceres's Name was on Honduran Military Hitlist, Says Former Soldier," *The Guardian*, June 21, 2016, www.theguardian.com/world/2016/jun/21/berta-caceres-name-honduran-military-hitlist-former-soldier

40 Ibid., Maya Rhodan, 2014.

41 TeleSUR, "Honduras: More Than 100 Lawyers Killed in Honduras in Five Years," August 11, 2016, https://videos.telesurtv.net/en/video/578451/honduras-more-than-100-lawyers-killed-in-honduras-in-five-years

42 Ibid., Nina Lakhani, "Did Hillary Clinton Stand by as Honduran Coup ushered in Era of Violence?" 2016.

43 Dana Frank, *The Long Honduran Night* (Chicago, IL: Haymarket Books, 2018). Frank notes that by 2016, ten women in Honduras were killed every week. Page 192

44 Committee to Protect Journalists, "Attacks on the Press in 2011: Honduras," https://cpj.org/2012/02/attacks-on-the-press-in-2011-honduras.php

45 *Global Witness*, "How Many More?" April 2015, www.globalwitness.org/en/campaigns/environmental-activists/how-many-more/

46 Politically active from a young age, in 1993 Berta Cáceres co-founded the Civic Council of Popular and Indigenous Organizations of Honduras (known by its Spanish abbreviation, COPINH).

47 Ibid., Nina Lakhani, 2016.

48 Cruz reportedly recognized Juan Galindo, an activist who had been in exile, but was assassinated in late 2014 when he returned to Honduras to visit his sick mother.

49 Lauren Carasik, "Honduran Activist's Murder Trial Addresses Symptoms, Not Causes, of Violence," *Foreign Policy*, December 7, 2018, https://foreignpolicy.com/2018/12/07/honduran-activist-murder-trial-addresses-symptoms-not-causes-of-violence/

50 Ibid., Nina Lakhani, 2016.

51 Ibid., Nina Lakhani, 2016.

52 Ibid., Lauren Carasik, 2018.

53 Ibid., Lauren Carasik, 2018.

54 Ibid., Alex Emmons, 2016.

55 Ioan Grillo, "'We won't Be Broken,' Caravan of Migrants Set Sights on U.S., Defying President Trump's Threats," *TIME*, October 21, 2018, http://time.com/5430436/migrant-caravan-mexico-guatemala-border/

56 Ibid., Ioan Grillo, 2018.

57 Ibid., Ioan Grillo, 2018.

58 Ibid., Dana Frank, 2018.

59 Sarah Chayes, "When Corruption is the Operating System: The Case of Honduras," *Carnegie Endowment for International Peace*, May 2016, https://carnegieendowment.org/2017/05/30/introduction-when-corruption-is-operating-system-case-of-honduras-pub-70000

60 Ibid., Sarah Chayes, 2017.
61 Ibid., Dana Frank, 2018, 192.
62 Ibid., Dana Frank, 2018, 191.
63 Ibid., Dana Frank, 2018, 192.
64 Honduras 2013 Human Rights Report, United States Department of State. https://webcache.googleusercontent.com/search?q=cache:eXlYibbj ZU4J:https://www.state.gov/documents/organization/220663. pdf+&cd=1&hl=en&ct=clnk&gl=us&client=firefox-b-1-d
65 "World Report 2014: Honduras," *Human Rights Watch*, www.hrw.org/ world-report/2014/country-chapters/honduras
66 *Democracy Now*, "It's not a Natural Disaster: Dana Frank on How US-Back Coup in Honduras Fueled Migrant Crisis," October 28, 2018, www.democracynow.org/2018/11/28/it_is_not_a_natural_disaster
67 Ibid., Dana Frank, *Democracy Now*, 2018.
68 Ibid., Dana Frank, *The Long Honduran Night*, 2018, 193.

4 Guatemala and the Extractive Industries

Media Fail to Connect Migrant Girl Who Died in CBP Custody to Years of Post-Colonial Oppression and Genocide

Robin Andersen

At the Border

On December 8, 2018, a 7-year-old Guatemalan girl named Jakelin died in the custody of U.S. Border Patrol agents. She was picked up in the early hours of December 6 with 163 other migrant who turned themselves into Custom and Border Protection CBP, in the remote desert borderlands of New Mexico. CBP officials delayed public notice of her death for a week. After that, Jakelin's story was widely reported, and as the details of the child's harrowing death came to light they spurred public outrage.[1] TV and press reported that her death was caused by dehydration, exhaustion, and finally cardiac arrest after falling into septic shock. Criticism of border patrol practices increased as the story unfolded.

NBC News started and ended a story with a picture of the tiny girl, dressed in blue denim standing in the low brush landscape of the desert.[2] She looked straight into the camera. Details of delayed medical care were followed by an interview with a humanitarian volunteer working in the desert. The young, blond woman wearing sunglasses and carrying a backpack standing in the sun was on screen for only a few seconds, and though quick editing prevented the sequence from making a coherent point, viewers saw a young woman criticizing current border policies. The story ended with a warning that such policies would lead to more deaths. On the defensive, Homeland Security Secretary Kirstjen Nielsen appeared on a Fox News broadcast saying Jakelin's family was responsible for "their choice to cross the border illegally."[3] Her comments fueled more criticism of border patrol policies.

The words of advocacy manager for the ACLU Border Rights Center, Cynthia Pompa, blaming the "lack of accountability, and a culture of cruelty within CBP" for the girl's death were published in the *Washington Post*. She went on to say that "The fact that it took a week for this to come to light shows the need for transparency for CBP." The ACLU called for a "rigorous investigation" in order to "prevent future deaths."[4]

As the coverage continued, earlier investigative reporting reentered the news cycle. The *Huffington Post* referenced a *ProPublica* report from 2017 that found "The number of migrant deaths rose by about 20 percent from 1998 to 2016, while the number of those captured crossing illegally plummeted 70 percent during the same period."[5] *ProPublica* had revealed the year before that the deaths of migrants crossing the desert were caused by CBP policies. "A significant source of the problem is the effort by authorities to deter migrants from using "easy-to-cross, hard-to-police urban corridors," and instead, they push them "into barren, isolated terrain," investigators wrote.[6] Weaponing the desert terrain as a deterrent policy had been taking its toll on migrants for years.

Once again we see that the crisis at the border, caused by the militarization of U.S. immigration policies, served to challenge security discourses. In the wake of Jakelin's death most news media expressed criticism and touched on basic humanitarian principles. The needless death of a small child evoked compassion, and the second death of another Guatemalan child, Felipe Gomez Alonso, on Christmas Eve, underscored the need for policy changes at the border. Felipe had been transferred among at least 4 facilities during the 6 days he was in custody.[7] Articles covering these deaths tapped into the language of humanitarian sensibilities. But only after the migrant caravan arrived at the U.S. borderlands did stories of hardship, death, and needless suffering emerge to challenge the dehumanized depictions of hordes and criminals ready to invade the country. Media coverage had finally begun to shift away from security discourses, but at a terrible cost.

In the weeks that followed, migrant images faded from television screens, and security policies reemerged once again as the dominant frame for reporting. As the stand-off between the House of Representatives and President Trump over funding for a border wall played out, no serious alternatives to security discourses entered the debate. Trump had set the terms—more security was needed—and that fundamental assertion held. Democrats did not question the claim that there was a "crisis of immigration."

Neither did they challenge the assertion that more security at the border was needed. No alternative policy platforms emerged to address border militarism, or the role of U.S. military policies in Central America. Instead, they simply argued that a border wall was not the best way to achieve security goals. Humanitarian language was once again overshadowed by political agreement on border security priorities.

As we have seen with media coverage about immigrants from El Salvador and Honduras, when covering the deaths of Jakelin and Felipe, conditions in Guatemala and the role the United States has played there were ignored in press accounts. A discussion of the reasons why Central Americans are forced to leave their homes would have set the parameters for a counter-narrative about immigration, which would have the potential for a meaningful public dialogue that could lead to change. However, historical background was omitted from most news accounts, with a few exceptions. *The Nation* magazine published articles written by two professors, and shined a light on the U.S. role in Guatemala. *Democracy Now* also picked up the story.

Jakelin's Death and the Long Struggle of the Indigenous People of Guatemala

Greg Grandin and Elizabeth Oglesby begin their piece in *The Nation* about the dead child with the words, "Her full name was Jakelin Amei Rosmery Caal Maquín, and she was from Guatemala."[8] In a little more than a thousand words the authors explain the historical roots of the crisis in Guatemala, a story that dates back even before the U.S.-backed military coup in 1954, and they bring it forward to the present day. Jakelin's was Q'eqchi' the indigenous term for Maya, from the town of Raxruhá, in the northern department of Alta Verapaz. Her father had tried his best to stay on his land, but since 2018 the wave of murders of Q'eqchi' peasant activists had made the situation dire. In addition, as the World Bank reported in 2003, the Q'eqchi' people are among the poorest of the poor in Guatemala, suffering from chronic malnutrition.[9] The World Food Program, which has been providing aid in Guatemala since 1974, reported that "poverty and extreme poverty rates (59 and 23 percent, respectively) increased between 2006 and 2014."[10] The consequences of extreme malnutrition result in the "stunting" of children, a phenomenon in Guatemala, is the fourth highest in the world and the highest in the region. But the Mayan people are not poor without reason. Jakelin died for these same reasons. Grandin and Oglesby explain what killed Jakelin, "The real killer was decades of US policy in support of Guatemalan regimes that have displaced and slaughtered the Maya population."[11]

What has happened in Guatemala since the CIA-orchestrated 1954 coup against the democratically elected government of Jacobo Arbenz[12] is much the same story that unfolded in Honduras after the 2009 military coup. The roots of the coup are also recognizable. Like Manuel Zelaya in Honduras, Jacob Arbenz had begun reforms in Guatemala that benefitted the Mayan farmers of Alta Verapaz. After the coup the military unleashed a wave of violence against the Mayan people. In the face of military attacks, the Q'eqchi's were forced to flee to the lowlands, in what is known as the "great migration." Raxruhá, Jakelin's home town, "was founded in the 1970s by these internal migrants."[13]

The Q'eqchi had struggled to stay on their lands in the fertile northern highlands of Guatemala since the early 1900s. They fought the coffee planters first, and later European and North American investors who also seized their lands through violence and legal manipulation. Jakelin is named after Adelina Caal Maquin, and like Jakelin, Adelina was a refugee who was forced to flee her mountain village for the lowlands. Adelina became a leader in the fight against the violent land evictions. In his book, *The Last Colonial Massacre: Latin American in the Cold War*, Grandin documents the killing of scores of protesters, a massacre that took place on May 29, 1978, known as the Panzós Massacre. Adelina Caal Maquin was also murdered that day.[14] In the years that followed, under the Reagan Administration's neo-cold war in Central America, over 100,000 Mayans would be killed by the U.S.-backed Guatemalan military.[15]

On March 23, 1982, General Efraín Ríos Montt, came to power through another military coup, and continued the war against the indigenous people of Guatemala. In *The Origins and Dynamics of Genocide*, Roddy Brett argues that Mayan insurgents were never a serious challenge to the government of General Ríos Montt, and that the military deliberately magnified the threat.[16] Far more civilians were killed than fighters, and because indigenous communities were specifically targeted based on ethnicity, Brett argues that the crimes against Guatemala's Indian communities amounted to genocide.[17] On May 10, 2013, Ríos Montt was convicted of genocide and crimes against humanity for trying to exterminate the Ixil indigenous group, a Mayan Indian community whose villages were wiped out by the military.[18] The decision made by a Guatemalan Tribunal was historic. It was the first time that a former head of state was tried in his own country for the crime of genocide. In a long piece that documents the road to justice taken in Guatemala, and details the evidence evaluated during the trial, author Marta Martinez emphasized that the trail "was the result of more than three decades of an unwavering fight for justice led by the victims and their families, activists and human rights defenders, lawyers and judges committed to their work."[19] Though the decision was overturned, Judge Yassmín Barrios, president of the three-judge tribunal that convicted Ríos Montt, remains steadfast about the importance of her tribunal's decision and the impact it had. The ruling, she said "lives in the heart of Guatemalans and of all citizens at an international level, because when dealing with a genocide case, it is aimed at the population of the whole world. It has validity."

After the death of Ríos Montt, writing in the *New York Times*, Stephen Kinzer reminded readers that Ronald Reagan was fond of the General, claiming that Ríos Montt was getting "a bum rap on human rights." Reagan asserted that Ríos Montt was "a man of great personal integrity and commitment. I know he wants to improve the quality of life for all Guatemalans and to promote social justice. My administration will do all it can to support his progressive efforts."[20]

Violence and environmental destruction continue to this day. In recent times, the Q'eqchi' suffer from the same multinational investment policies pushed by Washington that have killed and displaced so many environmental defenders in Honduras. A study by Alberto Alonso-Fradejas estimates that between 2003 and 2012, 11 percent of Q'eqchi' families lost their land to sugarcane and palm oil plantations.[21] The study supported by Food First concluded that, "powerful oil palm and sugarcane agribusinesses are grabbing lands farmed by Q'eqchi indigenous peasants who narrowly escaped the genocidal violence of the country's brutal civil war and bonded labor on large traditional estates." The report goes on to note that, "As such, the new wave of land grabs represents a tragic continuation in Guatemala's colonial and post-colonial history of subordination of the (indigenous) rural poor."[22] These global enterprises are financed by international institutions that enable the land grabs to take place.

In a series on sustainability, *Scientific America* includes Guatemala as an example of the way local farmers are being displaced worldwide to make way for the production of energy crop plantations.[23] Paramilitary forces working with Guatemalan soldiers have forcibly evicted hundreds of Mayan families so that transnational agribusiness, again financed by international institutions, can sell "energy crops" to global markets. Researcher Eitan Haddok writes,

> In early 2011 military and paramilitary forces forcibly evicted 13 communities of indigenous Mayan peasants—some 300 families were dispossessed of disputed land they had been living on for three years to secure the property rights of one powerful local family, the Widmanns, and its agribusiness company Chabil Utzaj.[24]

Haddok includes victim testimonials from those evicted, though names have been changed to prevent reprisals. "They don't respect anything or anyone, not even babies. We cried, there were shots and screaming." Haddok goes on to report that, "Further evictions are planned for villages and lands where these communities have been living for some 60 years."[25]

Because Guatemala, like Honduras, is a country rich in natural resources, the promotion of extractive industries such as mining, hydroelectric production, and timber logging has destroyed the subsistence economy of the Mayan people, poisoning their water and land. In the midst of such lawlessness in rural areas, Q'eqchi' communities have also become the victims of the escalating international drug war. Grandin and Oglesby writes, "Throughout the 2010s, drug-related crime and violence that had previously been concentrated in Colombia engulfed Central America, including Jakelin's birthplace accelerating migration north."[26] Q'eqchi' communities became transshipment points for cocaine moving into the United States. In the face of increasing brutality from drug traffickers and the repression of Q'eqchi' peasant activists by para-military forces, Guatemalans have been forced to leave their homelands.

This military, economic, political history of Guatemala is absent from U.S. reporting on the Central American refugee crisis. For example, NBC News aired a story filmed by the Associated Press of Jakelin's body being returned to the community and the small village where she lived. Though a reporter and camera crew were actually on the ground, no mention is made of the context detailed by Grandin and Oglesby, and other historians and researchers. With pictures of the small coffin and her mother crying beside it, the reporter describes the village this way: "The hamlet of about 420 people has no paved streets, running water or electricity, and residents say declining crop yields and lack of work have pushed many in the community to emigrate in recent years."[27] In this report, poverty comes from nowhere, it simply exists in a country U.S. viewers know virtually nothing about. No information that would complicate the narrative, or implicate the United States is uttered, and no mention is made of the multinational extractive industries that have seized the land of so many, and left other villages polluted, destroyed and lost to the people who once lived and farmed there. No background of the long struggle of the Mayan people is included, or the connections between Jakelin's iconic naming and the founding of the village where she was born.

Conclusion

The border deaths of two Guatemala children led to reporting critical of the militarized border patrol policies that killed them. Though news reports criticized security policies, and humanitarian concerns entered news coverage, when the news cycle moved forward, security discourses once again reemerged as the dominate discursive framework for news coverage of the border. Defining the Central American migration crisis as a crisis of immigration, instead of a crisis of border militarization and conditions in the region itself, held the discursive ground. The need for border security was underscored, instead of the need to change U.S. militarized policies in Central America, and to stop the further weaponization of the Southwestern borderlands of the United States.

The cycles of violence set in motion by U.S. interventions in the region—military adventures that, as Grandin points out, are usually on the wrong side of history—continue to destabilize the hemisphere, as it moves further away from peace and stability. Increasingly, violence at the border has gone hand-in-hand with the escalation of violence against immigrants in the United States. The growing number of right-wing patriot groups is currently at a 20-year high,[28] and violence by white supremacists has increased in the United States, fueled by the hate-filled speech that promises a wall between us and them. We will address these issues in the following chapter.

Notes

1 *New York* magazine reports, for example,

> About eight hours after being taken into custody—before Border Patrol transferred the asylum-seekers to a station in Lordsburg, New Mexico—Nery Caal reported to officials that his daughter was vomiting and running a high fever—later charted at 105.9. Officials reportedly ignored his concerns for a full hour-and-a-half.

See Amanda Arnold, "Everything We Know about 7-Year-Old Migrant Girl Who Dies in Custody," December 17, 2018, www.thecut. com/2018/12/jakelin-caal-7-year-old-migrant-girl-died-border-control. html

2 Julia Ainsley, Jacob Soboroff, and Cal Perry, "7-Year Old Dies in Border Patrol Custody," NBC News, December 15, 2019, NBC, www. nbcnews.com/politics/immigration/seven-year-old-girl-who-died-border-did-not-receive-n948071

3 Fox News, December 14, 2018.

4 Nick Miroff and Robert Moore, "7-Year Old Migrant Girl Taken into Border Patrol Custody Died of Dehydration, Exhaustion," *Washington Post*, December 13, 2018, www.washingtonpost.com/world/national-security/7-year-old-migrant-girl-taken-into-border-patrol-custody-dies-of-dehydration-exhaustion/2018/12/13/8909e356-ff03-11e8-862a-b6a6f3ce8199_story.html?utm_term=.226d0fab0d89

5 George Joseph, "Why Do Border Deaths Persist When the Number of Border Crossings is Falling," *ProPublica*, September 17, 2017, www.pro publica.org/article/why-do-border-deaths-persist-when-the-number-of-border-crossings-is-falling

6 Amy Russo, "DHS Secretary Blames Migrant Family for Childs HarrowingDeath," *HuffingtonPost*, December 14, 2018, www.huffington post.com/entry/dhs-secretary-migrant-child-death-response_us_5c13de2ce4b05d7e5d81b44f

7 Miriam Jordan, "'A Breaking Point,' Second Child's Death Prompts New Procedures for Border Agency," *New York Times*, December 26, 2018, www.nytimes.com/2018/12/26/us/felipe-alonzo-gomez-customs-border-patrol.html

8 Greg Grandin and Elizabeth Oglesby, "Who Killed Jakelin Caal Maquín at the US Border?" *The Nation*, December 12, 2018, www. thenation.com/article/guatemala-refugee-crisis-jakelin-caal-maquin/

9 Alessandra Marini and Michele Gragnolati, Malnutrition and Poverty in Guatemala, Policy Research Working Paper, *The World Bank*, January 2003, http://webcache.googleusercontent.com/search?q=cache:1 RO53fj74GsJ:siteresources.worldbank.org/EXTLACREGTOPNUT/Resources/Guatemala_nurtition_WPS2967.pdf+&cd=1&hl=en&ct=clnk&gl=us&client=firefox-b-1-d

10 World Food Program, "WFP: Guatemala: Country Brief," June, 2018, www1.wfp.org/countries/guatemala

11 Ibid., Greg Grandin and Elizabeth Oglesby, 2018.

12 Kate Doyle and Peter Kornbluh, eds., "CIA and Assassinations: The Guatemala 1954 Documents," *The National Security Archive*, https://nsarchive2.gwu.edu/NSAEBB/NSAEBB4/

13 Ibid., Greg Grandin and Elizabeth Oglesby, 2018.

14 Greg Grandin, *The Last Colonial Massacre: Latin America in the Cold War, Updated Edition*, Naomi Klein, contributor (Chicago, IL: University of Chicago Press, 2011).

15 Greg Grandin, "Guatemalan Slaughter was part of Reagan's Hard Line", *New York Times*, May 21, 2013, www.nytimes.com/roomfordebate/2013/05/19/what-guilt-does-the-us-bear-in-guatemala/guatemalan-slaughter-was-part-of-reagans-hard-line

16 Roddy Brett, *The Origins and Dynamics of Genocide* (New York: Palgrave Macmillan, 2016).

17 World Peace Foundation: Atrocities, Guatemala, August 7, 2015, https://sites.tufts.edu/atrocityendings/2015/08/07/guatemala/

18 Stephen Kinzer, "Efraín Ríos Montt, Guatemalan Dictator Convicted of Genocide, Dies at 91," *New York Times*, April 1, 2018, www.nytimes.com/2018/04/01/obituaries/efrain-rios-montt-guatemala-dead.html

19 Marta Martinez, "Impunity's Eclipse: The Long Journey to the Historic Genocide Trial in Guatemala," *The International Center for Transitional Justice* (ICTJ), www.ictj.org/sites/default/files/subsites/guatemala-genocide-impunity-eclipse/

20 Ibid., Kinzer, 2018.

21 Alberto Alonso-Fradejas, "'Sons and Daughters of the Earth': Indigenous communities and land grabs in Guatemala" (Land & Sovereignty in the Americas Series, No. 1), in *Food First/Institute for Food and Development Policy and Transnational Institute*, Oakland, CA, 2013, www.tni.org/files/download/land-sov_series_briefs_-_ndcg1_alonso-fradejas_final.pdf

22 Ibid., Alberto Alonso-Fradejas, 2013.

23 Eitan Haddok, "Biofuels Land Grab: Guatemala's Farmers Lose Plots and Prosperity to 'Energy Independence,'" *Scientific American*, January 13, 2012, www.scientificamerican.com/article/biofuels-land-grab-guatemala/

24 Ibid., Eitan Haddok, 2012.

25 Ibid., Eitan Haddok, 2012. He include other testimonials, "They came in great numbers and heavily armed," says 18-year-old Tecla Kuxh while holding her one-year-old infant, via a translator.

26 Ibid., Greg Grandin and Elizabeth Oglesby, 2018.

27 Associated Press, "Body of Migrant Girl Who Died in U.S. Border Patrol Custody Arrives Home in Guatemala," December 24, 2018, www.nbcnews.com/news/latino/body-migrant-girl-who-died-u-s-border-patrol-custody-n951656

28 Kelly Macias, "In 2018, the Number of Hate Groups in America Reached a 20-year High—Thanks to Trump," *Daily Kos*, February 27, 2019, www.dailykos.com/stories/2019/2/21/1836592/-In-2018-the-number-of-hate-groups-in-America-reached-a-twenty-year-high-thanks-to-Trump?detail=emailLL

5 Violence and Brutality at the U.S. Border and Beyond

The Media and the Perpetuation of Militarism in the Hemisphere

Robin Andersen

A Crisis of Security or a Huamitarian Crisis of Compassion and Policy?

Let us now connect the histories of the countries of the Northern Triangle detailed in previous chapters to what has been repeatedly identified by the President, other politicians, and many in the press as an immigration crisis at the U.S. Border. Tying these strings together will offer an alternative view to the media frames based in fear and the alarmist discourses of security that undergird the language of immigration. Security discourses succeed in transforming innocent refugees fleeing violence—violence that we are in large measure responsible for—into dehumanized criminals, which allows us to continue to brutalize them in the name of national security. But what price do we pay for our own loss of humanity as we watch the effects of militarization on innocent refugees, or worse, turn our gaze away from those who suffer? To answer this question, we begin with an assessment of what is actually happening in the deserts of the Southwestern borderlands of the United States. We will draw on the writings of Francisco Cantu (among others), who grapples with the innumerable ways that violence becomes normalized in the liminal spaces of the borderlands, and increasingly in the border communities themselves. Cantu, who authored a memoir titled *The Line Becomes a River*, was a Border Patrol Guard for over a decade. He writes "Violence does not grow organically in our deserts, it has arrived there through policy."[1] By extension, what is happening on the border is happening to us all, even if we fail to see it. That violence has now taken hold in the United States. This is more likely the nexus of the real crisis we are experiencing today.

In this volume, we have looked back historically to understand the forced migrations from Central America's Northern Triangle, and the multiple ways in which media coverage fails to illuminate the history and causes of those migrations. The words of Francisco Cantú acknowledge that the current politics of U.S. immigration at the border has a historical genesis.

> To describe what we are seeing as a "crisis," however, is to imply that our current moment is somehow more horrifying than those that have recently set the stage for it—moments that, had we allowed ourselves to see them and be horrified by them, might have prevented our arrival here in the first place.[2]

We will start with an account of the current illegal immigration into the United States.

A False Crisis

As we documented in Chapter 2, though media repeat political assertions that the border is in crisis, by any metric used to measure illegal entry into the United States, the overall scale of unlawful immigration is at a historic low. Today there are many fewer migrants entering the U.S. illegally than at any time in recent history. For example in 2017, 415,000 migrants were apprehended near the border, the lowest since 1970 and 77.1 percent lower than the peak of 1,815,000 in 2000. The number of those who manage to enter the country illegally has also shrunk precipitously. According to the Department of Homeland Security, between 2006 and 2016, "estimated undetected unlawful entries fell from approximately 851,000 to nearly 62,000 ..., a 93 percent decrease."[3] Thirdly, policies instituted by successive administrations have led to mass deportations. Far more Central Americans and others are being deported, first under the Clinton era Illegal Immigration Reform and Immigrant Responsibility Act of 1996 and in the wake 9/11, the Bush Administration's Homeland Security Act of 2002. Actions taken by the Obama Administration also led to a decrease in the number of illegal migrations in the US. In the summer of 2014, a surge of 68,000 unaccompanied minors arrived at the U.S. border fleeing horrific violence in the countries of the Northern Triangle, with the greatest proportion arriving from Honduras. The youth had been forced to flee because of the worsening conditions in the U.S.-backed Honduran tyrannical regime.

The Obama administration took unprecedented measures to stop them, and two years later that number dropped by half and "the crisis" receded from the headlines. But the numbers did not decline because the violence in Central America stopped, or because its victims were not forced to flee. The Obama Administration had outsourced border security to Mexico, providing millions of dollars in equipment and training to the Mexican government to halt the flow of immigrants across its southern border with Guatemala and Belize.[4] Alternative media covered the outsourcing story infrequently, but in *The Intercept* in 2016, Woodhouse wrote, "Apprehensions in Mexico have gone up by 71 percent without an accompanying expansion of screenings for legitimate asylum claims." He went on to point out that these policies led to the increased suffering of young people who were already the victims of violence and brutality:

> As a result, many refugees are being summarily deported back to the countries they fled—countries in which they have been personally targeted for murder, rape, and gang conscription— before ever having a chance to present their claims for asylum before an American immigration judge. In the meantime, they're warehoused in prisons and treated by American immigration courts as if they were the violent gangsters they risked their lives to escape.[5]

After the crisis of unaccompanied minors became prominent in the media in 2014, public discourse became increasingly anti-immigration.[6] Reports failed to connect the causes of forced migrations, the treatment of immigrants, or the inhumane militarization of border policies into a coherent explanatory perspective that would point to the need for change, and a different set of policies. The militarization of the hemisphere continued to escalate at a rapid pace, in a long historical build up that continues today. Deteriorating living conditions and the threat of imminent death have pushed Central Americans north, and those conditions amount to the crises that started well before migrants reached the border.

From Fighting "Communism" in Central America to the "War on Drugs" in the Northern Triangle

Almost exactly 30 years after the coup in El Salvador that led to the U.S.-backed civil war, the United States would choose once again, a repressive military regime in Central America over the people's demands for justice and democracy. What happened in Honduras has re-set the United States on a course that repeats past policy failures, and increases brutality across the hemisphere. Writing in *The Intercept*, Jake Johnston calls The 2009 military coup in Honduras a "a brazen display of 1970s behavior in the 21st century."[7] He writes that a retired U.S. military officer told him, on conditions of anonymity, that when coup supporters debated how to manage the United States, they decided to "start using the true and trusted method and say, 'Here is the bogeyman, it's communism.'"[8] In addition, Johnston documents how a network of former Cold Warriors and Republicans in Congress "loudly encouraged Honduras's de facto regime." One army Colonel who helped perpetrate the coup claimed that Zelaya "was simply an acolyte of Venezuelan President Hugo Chávez, public enemy No. 1 of the U.S. in the hemisphere." Another member of the Honduran army told the *Miami Herald* a few days after the coup, that "It would be difficult for us, with our training, to have a relationship with a leftist government. That's impossible."[9] The United States adopted this narrative and revived Cold War policies, even though the historical record, the literature of Latin America, and the scholars who study the region have documented the war's brutality and demonstrated the failures of militarism to secure peace and stability. Using Guatemala as his case study for example, in *The Last Colonial Massacre*, Greg Grandin concludes that the Cold War in Latin American was not a struggle between political liberalism and Soviet Communism. Instead he details the ways in which the wealthy oligarchs and political reactionaries held on to their power and privilege through military force. When challenged by Mayan Marxists, they simply labeled them communists, but the community response to violence and oppression was undergirded with a philosophical blend of "indigenous notions of justice with universal ideas of equality."[10] Indeed these fundamentally humanitarian concepts have been codified in international human rights formulations for half a century. But as we will see below, the United States reacted to insurgencies by supporting repression and actively developing and exporting new styles of state terror to battle community responses to oppression.[11]

As policies pivot back to the failures of the 1970s and 1980s, the justifications and arguments presented to Congress and the American people for the continued funding of repressive military regimes has changed. The fight is no longer against communism.

Now the United States is fighting "drug cartels and gang violence." Such justifications are equally specious, though the consequences of increased brutality and violence are real.

Human Rights Violations and the War on Drugs

As we documented in Chapter 3, the people of Honduras have been resisting military force since 2009, resulting in untold suffering with many pushed off their land, beaten, brutalized, and killed by military and para-military forces working on behalf of global elites and multinational corporations. As Dana Frank documents in her book, *The Long Honduran Night*, since the coup, government corruption has dismantled the rule of law, leaving the police, the judiciary, and the courts unable to stop the violence or prosecute those responsible for it. But news coverage of the ongoing crisis taking place inside Honduras is overshadowed by the "crisis" at the U.S. border. Media accept uncritically the claim that funding the Honduran military is necessary to fight the war on drugs, gangs violence, and illegal immigration. But the violence only escalates. Many of these same dynamics are mirrored in Guatemala, where indigenous communities are once again pushed off their homelands, this time to make way for "bio-fuel production," and a host of agro and extractive industries. In El Salvador, the brutal gang M-13 grew out of the interconnected consequences of the U.S.-backed civil war, a country that has not recovered from that destruction and brutality. Politicians use the threat of gang violence to stay in power and receive U.S. military support, even though experience demonstrates that peaceful negotiations work, and that brutality and human rights violations do not.

Citing the flow of drugs as a rationale, Johnston observes, "the U.S. government gave at least $57 million in military aid to Honduras between 2009 and 2014," in addition to the tens of millions of dollars the U.S. military spends on contracts in Honduras.[12] And *The Guardian* reported that Honduras has long been a strategic partner for Washington: since 2009, the United States has invested nearly $114 million in security assistance to establish elite military and police units, ratchet up border security, and carry out counter-narcotics operations as part of Hernández's crackdown on gangs.[13]

In the book *Base Nation*, David Vine details the way U.S. aid maintains at least 13 military bases in the country, three of which were built after the coup. Indeed, more than 600 U.S. troops remain in Honduras as part of a program called "Joint Task Force

Bravo," where U.S. Special Forces help train their Honduran coun-terparts.[14] Indeed, the *Wall Street Journal* published a video report in 2016 showing Green Berets teaching Honduran soldiers how to raid homes.[15] The sensationalized combat-heavy footage used night vision shots of soldiers lining up poor residents in the town of Habitat, just outside the capital of Tegucigalpa. In the middle of the night, individuals are forced to stand against a wall as the voice over claims the suspects are gangs members, yet no drugs or guns are found on the compliant targets of police harassment. Viewers are offered no proof of gang association, as the reporter intones, this is "the most dangerous place on earth." The reporter also ad-mits that this training in part of a "little-known" campaign, and claims the "training will help Honduras combat gang violence." Children are not visible, but their crying can be heard off camera. No mention is made of the well-known fact that the criminal justice system had long been dismantled, leaving the corrupt Honduran police to act with impunity. By 2013, 70 percent of the police were corrupt, paid off or themselves engaged in organized crime, "in-cluding trafficking, extortion, rape, and murder for hire."[16]

A militarized Honduras is where the United States now stages its interventions into the rest of Central America, and is planning to do more so in the future.

The Media Myth of Fighting Drug Cartels

The day after *Reuters'* photojournalist Kim Kyung-Hoon took the photograph of the migrant mother at the border in San Ysidro, U.S. federal prosecutors announced charges against Juan Antonio Hernandez, a former Honduran congressman and the younger brother of Juan Orlando Hernández, the current president of Honduras. Prosecutors described the brother as "a 'large-scale drug trafficker' who spent a dozen years moving cocaine shipments bound for the United States through Central America." The *New York Times* cited Geoffrey S. Berman, the United States attorney in Manhattan, saying that Juan Antonio was deeply involved in the drug trade. He arranged security, took bribes from traffickers, and acquired "government contracts for money-laundering front companies."[17]

Information included in the article reveals the strong ties be-tween drug trafficking and the corruption and malfeasants of the government of Honduras. For example, Hernández paid off law enforcement officials, "on behalf of one or more high-ranking

Honduran politicians." The indictment also charges Hernández with "transporting and distributing multi-ton loads of cocaine into Honduras via planes, go-fast vessels, and on at least one occasion, **a submarine**." [emphasis added] Hernandez also took bribes to ensure that "Honduran government agencies would make payments owed to front companies they operated to launder drug money."[18] And finally, a leader of one drug cartel who testified against Hernandez, had also provided evidence that convicted Fabio Lobo of drug trafficking, the son of the president in power after the 2009 coup, Porfirio Lobo. In 2016, InSight Crime documented the ways in which Fabio Lobo profited from drug trafficking, trading off of his lucrative government ties.[19]

Even in the face of such damning details of post-coup government corruption, clearly tied to drug trafficking, the *Times* is mild in its criticism, and fails to connect the story to failed U.S. military policies. The *Times* uses language such as "tarnished the reputation" of the Honduran state, saying the arrest has "cast an unwanted spotlight on the influence" of drug traffickers, and that President Hernández, is an "ally of the United States" who has "staked his credibility on the fight against organized crime."[20] One sentence connects the story to out migration. "It also underscores the entrenched corruption in Honduran law enforcement agencies at a time when thousands of Hondurans are fleeing the countries violence and poverty to seek asylum in the United States."[21] Yet no acknowledgement is made of U.S. involvement is dismantling the rule of law, or the criminal justice system in Honduras. There are no follow-up questions or reporting about corrupt Honduran politicians, or the business and financial support needed for drug cartels. No acknowledgement that drug trafficking is part of the family business for successive Honduran Presidents supported by funding allocated for the war on drugs. Reporting in other news outlets was much the same. Though the arrest was covered on major media from CNN to the *New York Post*, and even by the BBC, most quote the Honduran President, claiming justice will prevail and reassuring the public that the government remains "committed to the fight against drug trafficking and corruption." This BBC story ends with the warning that justifies the war on drugs, "Honduras is a major transit route for cocaine smuggled from Colombia and other South American nations to the US."[22]

Had the *New York Times* referenced its own op-ed piece published a year earlier, it could have connected the arrest to what Silvio Carrillo wrote in "America's Blind Eye to Honduras's

Tyrant."[23] Carrillo, the nephew of murdered environmental activist Berta Cáceres, offers ample evidence of corruption, and extends a plea to the United States to stop funding the brutal government of Juan Orlando Hernández. In the face of well-documented human rights abuses and political bribery, Carrillo details how Hernández held on to power through another stolen election in 2017. In the face of protest, the American Embassy's chargé d'affaires asked the Honduran people to be calm. "This played right into Mr. Hernández's hands; he declared a state of emergency and imposed martial law, securing for himself a wide berth to use Honduras's American-trained security forces to repress the opposition." With the help of a Washington-based public relations firm, Keybridge Communication, Hernández successfully blamed ensuing violence on the opposition, even though Amnesty International reported that state security forces had fired live rounds and killed over a dozen people during peaceful protests against the failed electoral process.[24] Amnesty International goes on to say, "Honduras seems to be on a very dangerous free fall where ordinary people are the victims of reckless and selfish political games."[25] On November 28, two days after the failed election, the "State Department certified that Honduras had made progress in protecting human rights and attacking corruption." Millions of dollars in military funding were released to the Hernández government.[26]

Media, Gang Violence, and Drug Cartels

On the same day the picture of the migrant mother was taken, *60 Minutes* on CBS aired an expose of the Trump Administration's family separation policy, roundly condemning the inhumane treatment of refugees. Included were interviews with health-care professionals and others appalled by the policies and long-term harm they are doing to refugees and their families. The broadcast features footage of a photogenic 3-year-old boy who was separated from his father after he crossed the border, reporting that "Immers and his father crossed the border illegally but presented themselves to the Border Patrol and requested asylum." The show explains why Ever and his son Immers were forced to flee their home. Ever was shot in the back in Honduras, *a country at war with gangs and drug cartels*."[27] [emphasis added]. But neither the government, the security forces, the elite, nor law enforcement in the country of Honduras are at war with gangs. As confirmed by numerous writers and analysts, the Honduran regime is part of the international drug trade and profits from gang activities nurtured by government corruption and the dismantling of democracy. But in media narratives about Central American refugees, "gang violence and drug cartels" are used as a short hand, distilled, and simplified into an all-encompassing explanation. They stand alone, nothing needs to be added to these iconic evils emerging from nowhere. As an ill-defined force, drug and gang violence now occupy a mythic realm, yet one immediately recognized as an iconic source of all evil. Like a "natural disaster" or "human nature," they simply exist. Because no coherent background contextualizes how such organizations took hold in the Northern Triangle, and have flourished under repressive governments, themselves connected to the trade, and supported by the U.S. military, "gang violence and drug traffickers" can stand alone even when reporting openly contradicts and exposes these policy myths. The origins of violence, and the lawlessness of U.S.-supported governments deeply interwoven into hemispheric violence is rarely the subject of expository narratives about Central America. Journalists make no mention that gangs and drug cartels grew out of the failed policies and funding priorities set in place by successive administrations in Washington, D.C.

Migrants, Refugees, and Economics

When explanations are given for why so many Central Americans are seeking to enter the United States, they are primarily identified as economic—people are looking for jobs and a more prosperous lifestyle. As Geraldo Rivera said on the Fox News program *The Five*:

> We are a nation of immigrants. These are desperate people. They walked 2,000 miles. Why? Because they want to rape your daughter or steal your lunch? No. Because they want a job!...

Like violence that comes from nowhere, poverty is also simply endemic. No context explains how Honduran and Guatemalan migrants became so impoverished in countries where wealthy elites thrive on the extraction of rich natural resources. No background illuminating how funding from the United States supports military and paramilitary security policies that force people from community lands and subsistence farming into poverty. Identifying refugees as simply economic migrants obscures what is at stake for those fleeing targeted violence in their home countries.

Yet, poor people have crossed borders to improve their lives for centuries. Criminalizing economic immigrants is equally brutal and inhumane.[28] We will argue for alternative narratives and immigration policies in the following chapter.

Immigration, The Border Patrol Agency, U.S. Law Enforcement, and the Militarization of the U.S. Borderlands

Just as the destabilizing of the countries of Central America has a long history in U.S. foreign policy, so too, the militarization of the United States borderlands dates back to earlier times, and is connected to U.S. policies in the hemisphere. Trump's demonization of illegal immigrants, "othered," as people of color and charged with being "criminals" and "rapists," may be considered only the most recent outcome of a process set in place much earlier. In the book *Boats, Borders, and Bases*, the authors date current immigration discourse to policies that criminalized migration in the 1980s.[29] Efforts to prevent the arrival of asylum seekers built upon domestic crime politics of the time that labeled "inner city youth" deviant and criminal during the war on drugs. Young black men in urban areas became the targets of law enforcement, not financial institutions that laundered drug money, or white suburban consumers of drugs. Media celebrated the war on drugs through docu-cop programs like *Cops* that aired for years on Fox network.[30] Authors Loyd and Mountz identify the interrelationships between the domestic expansion of jails and prisons, and the extension of military bases to show how "the location of migration detention commonly builds on prison and military geographies."[31] Though the United States currently maintains the world's largest migration and deportation system, there has been little systematic research or reporting devoted to understanding the emergence or consequences of this system. The current acceleration of military logics and priorities in the borderlands are an extreme outward expansion of border policies set in motion years ago.

Grandin and Oglesby trace current border patrol practices back even further, to the agency's establishment in the early 1990s, when it operated with near impunity and became "arguably the most politicized branch of federal law enforcement."[32] The authors detail some of the Cold War history, making direct connections between the agency and U.S. military policies in

Central America, when border patrol tactics were exported to Guatemala and other anticommunist regimes. One U.S. Border Patrol agent, John Longan, worked near the Mexican border in the 1940s and 1950s,[33] and during his time he acquired a reputation for violence. During the height of the cold war in the mid-1960s, the United States recruited Logan to provide "security assistance to allied anticommunist nations." Grandin and Oglesby write, "Put simply, Longan taught local intelligence and police agencies how to create death squads to target political activists, deploying tactics that he'd used earlier to capture migrants on the border." While he was in Guatemala, Logan established a paramilitary unit that carried out Operación Limpieza, or Operation Cleanup.

> Within three months, this unit conducted over 80 raids and multiple assassinations, including an action that, over the course of four days, led to the capture, torture, and execution of more than 30 prominent left-wing opposition leaders. The military dumped their bodies into the sea, while the government denied any knowledge of their whereabouts.[34]

In Stuart Schrader's forthcoming book *Badges Without Borders: How Global Counterinsurgency Transformed American Policing*, he documents the practice of sending former Border Patrol agents to train foreign police through CIA-linked "public safety" programs, which helped security forces target and kill political reformers.[35] Speaking on *CounterSpin*, the radio program produced by the media watch group Fairness and Accuracy in Reporting (FAIR), writer and journalist Jon Swartz referred to the brutality experienced over the years by the people of Guatemala as "unspeakable horrors," actions so difficult to describe that words fail to communicate their true impact.[36]

The shared military tactics between the Border Patrol and counterinsurgency in the Americas has led to a sub-culture of cruelty along the U.S. southern borderlands and fueled hostility to migrants and Latin Americans. Paramilitary organizations increased in number in the twenty-first century, becoming better organized and more vicious. Patrolling began to attract soldiers who had returned from the war on terror, as well as veterans of older conflicts. In 2004, the Minuteman Project, which began patrolling the desert in search of illegal immigrants, was founded by a Vietnam veteran named Jim Gilchrist.

The Minuteman Project and the Media

In 2004, the Minuteman Project was launched, with a mission to patrol the U.S.-Mexico border in search of illegal border cross-ers. The project is a twenty-first century manifestation of the anti-immigration movement that flourished in the United States since the late 1980s.[37] In April 2005, the vigilante organization staged its first major operation, sending 200 members to guard seven outposts that stretched 23 miles along of the Arizona-Mexico border. Minutemen arrived camera ready and heavily equipped, dressed in fatigues with military garb, like "binoculars, bullet-proof vests, aircraft, walkie-talkie and even guns."[38] Their ob-jective went beyond simply capturing undocumented immi-grants. They had set their sights on the media, and it worked. Reporters turned up in full force. *Los Angeles Times* journalist David Kelly wrote, "The number of media members to cover the volunteer border patrols nearly outnumbered the Minute-men. Reporters from around the world descended on Tombstone. Along with journalists came filmmakers working on documenta-ries about the U.S.-Mexico border."[39] Gilchrist was quick to claim success. "We have already accomplished our goal a hundred-fold in getting the media out here and getting the message out."[40] The ACLU charged the organization with disseminating mis-information and acknowledged that it had successfully ma-nipulated the media.[41] Leo Chavez identifies the Minuteman Project's media strategy as a performative spectacle of surveil-lance.[42] In addition, Michelle Holling found that the Minuteman Project successfully constructed an identity that resonated with themes of patriotism, masculinity, and militarism, while mask-ing the "white supremacist values undergirding" the Project. [43] The group also successfully framed undocumented immigrants as invaders, and identified them as "dehumanized, externalized, and criminalized subjects."[44] Research by Joshua Grimm, also found that television picked up on the theme of whiteness, using it as an implicit yet dominant frame. On TV news, "whiteness remained invisible while the threat toward whiteness became pronounced.[45] Building on Grimm's analysis, Cynthia Van Der Heyden found that media reinforced these frames, presenting the Minuteman Project through "hegemonic notions of whiteness" that remained unchallenged throughout "the media coverage of this racial is-sue."[46] She concludes her analysis of television news saying that "through effective framing and misinformation," television news "either willfully or unconsciously, contributed to, if not made the success of the Minuteman Project."[47] Media played an important part in the early weaponization of anti-immigration extremists and helped position the movement within the mainstream of U.S. media discourse. These themes resonate today in the rhetorics of nativist fear-inducing, anti-immigration narratives.

By the end of 2004, Minuteman mania had spread across the country. The Associated Press reported that at least 40 anti-immigration groups popped up nationally, inspired by the Minutemen who had successfully staged border patrols.[48] Media coverage helped generate the growth of affiliated chapters in 18 states from California to places like Utah, Minnesota, and Maine. A California group urged its "volunteers" to bring "baseball bats, Mace, pepper spray and machetes to patrol the border." But eventually the vigilant group settled on guns, as one Minuteman explained, "to keep my people alive."[49] Escalating rhetoric and the demonization of Hispanics marked the growth of the vigilante movement. For example, the influence of the Tennessee Minutemen evoked misinformation and scapegoating, when one official suggested that immigrants were to blame if property taxes had to be raised.[50] In Knoxville, a spokesperson with Alianza del Pueblo, a regional Hispanic support group, worried that the group was terrorizing the community.

Since then, the media have played a significant role in popularizing and even celebrating vigilantism, and the worst anti-immigration perspectives that turn migrants into human prey for national entertainment through reality TV shows.

A Culture of Cruelty; "Human Prey" and "Border Porn"

Over the years, the border has become a terrain often occupied by white supremacist and their attendant violence, giving voice to racist and nativist fantasies. Greg Grandin ties the perpetuation of such fantasies to the often sensationalized media representations of those who stalk the border.[51] In the early days of Fox News during the 1990s, the network aired a show called *The Reporters*. In one episode titled "Human Prey," cameras track a group of high school students who mascaraed as a neo-Nazi paramilitary group, calling themselves the Metal Militia.[52] They stage "war games," hunting down and robbing migrants.[53] One vigilante estimated that there were about 10 militant groups in the San Diego County area who would "hunt, track, and stalk" migrants for sport.[54]

"Human Prey" launched a new genre of TV shows that Grandin calls "border patrol porn." Well before Donald Trump became national news, National Geographic channel ran five seasons of *Border Wars*. Discovery Channel followed suit with *Border Live* and Netflix with *Border Security*, shows that mirror the style of Docu- *Cops,* where cameras look over the shoulders of law enforcement.[55] This version of "reality" follows Border Patrol agents as they surveille the desert. Camera perspectives allow viewers to experience the exhilarating power of the chase, enhanced by greenish night-vision cinematography, and other militainment strategies[56] that feature doors being battered down, Black Hawk helicopters, and jeeps speeding through mesquite scrub. While driving, Border Patrol agents wearing dark sunglasses "hold forth on life, duty, manhood, and their occasional doubts."[57]

One particularly disturbing episode of *Border Wars*, titled "Lost in the River,"[58] features exciting footage of helicopters and all-terrain vehicles being used to scatter migrants, forcing them into fast flowing rivers, or deeper into the deadly desert terrain. Many must simply disappear or die, either from drowning or dehydration.

> It's a game—patrollers play scatter, chase, catch; migrants surrender or die—that pits desperate people with next to no resources against one of the best-funded, high-tech, armed-to-the-teeth law enforcement agencies on earth. "We'll let him tire himself out. If he wants to run, we'll let him run... It's a never-ending game for us."[59]

Grandin makes some chilling connections between the shows and the loss of compassion in an age of Empire.

> Watching such spectacles on cable TV, it's hard not to feel that the United States is now ancient Rome—an empire that, in its later years, held compassion to be a vice—and the whole of that southwestern desert our Colosseum.[60]

On April 19, 2019, CBS News carried a story about a vigilante group calling itself the United Constitutional Patriots operating in New Mexico along the U.S.-Mexico Border. The group had detained 300 people who were seeking safety in the United States. CBS quoted the ACLU calling for an "official probe" saying "We cannot allow racist and armed vigilantes to kidnap and detain people seeking asylum."[61] Documentation by the ACLU was picked up by other major media outlets, and marks an important moment for critical coverage of border vigilantism and militarization.

The Brutal Treatment of Refugees

The day after Trump was elected President, writer Stephen Hopsgood warned that if Trump's proposed immigration policies were implemented, "deaths and killings in custody, border firefights and lacerating misery are almost inevitable."[62] These words indeed describe what has come to pass.

The worst of it started one year into Trump's administration. In April 2018, Attorney General Jeff Sessions announced an immigration policy of "zero tolerance," saying all adults who cross the border illegally would be criminally prosecuted. This policy caused a cascade of human rights abuses.[63] Since children can't be sent to jail, detained children would be separated from their parents.[64] Kids were handed over to the U.S. Department of Health and Human Services' Office of Refugee Resettlement. By the middle of June, at least 2,500 children were being held in custody.[65]

Now, for the first time, migrants arriving at the border, including people coming to seek asylum, face criminal prosecution. More than 30,000 migrants have been convicted through July. One newspaper noted the irony, "President Trump has long claimed that people who cross the border illegally are criminals. Now, thanks to zero tolerance, a growing number of them are."[66] California Attorney General Xavier Becerra made news as one of the few prominent democrats to challenge the criminalization of immigrants. "They are not criminals," Becerra said of migrants who cross without authorization. "They haven't committed a crime against someone, and they are not acting violently or in a way that's harmful to people. And I would argue they are not harming people indirectly either."[67]

Press reports began to detail the ensuing brutality, and even death, all along this chain from apprehension to incarceration— from small children screaming and crying when yanked from their parents, to infants dying in custody. One undocumented migrant mother from Honduras sobbed as she described to an attorney how federal agents wrenched her daughter away from her as she was breastfeeding. Natalia Cornelio, the attorney with the Texas Civil Rights Project, reported that when the woman resisted, she was handcuffed.[68] Some parents who are under arrest tell public defenders they don't know what happened to their children. The violence against border crossers mirrors the worst historical treatment of innocent, demonized people. One story resonates with the Nazi roundup of Jews on their way to concentration camps. At the U.S. border, some parents were told their children were being taken to be bathed or cleaned up, and the adults never saw them again.[69]

The conditions of detention for adults and children forced to flee the violence in their home countries, are equally brutal and inhuman.

Immigration and Customs Enforcement (ICE) reported that nearly 50,000 migrants are in custody, but observers who have seen the facilities use the word "incarcerated." The Department of Health and Human Services admits that "The total number of children separated from a parent or guardian by immigration authorities is unknown." Children are housed in overcrowded facilities, stacked in bunks on top of one another,[70] or worse on floors in chain-link cells covered only with a thin, metallic blanket. They use desert tents and make-shift prisons, and are so understaffed that children are dispensed phototrophic drugs to keep them quite.[71] They eat in shifts, sometimes also on floors, are forced to drink water from toilets, and medical care is withheld. In August 2018, NPR reported the needless death due to repertory failure of an 18-month-old named Mariee Juárez after being held in Dilley, Texas.[72]

A damning report released in May 2018 by the ACLU exposed the "culture of impunity," within U.S. Customs and Border Protection and the Department of Homeland Security.[73] Based on more than 30,000 pages of documents obtained through the Freedom of Information Act, the report describes the "pervasive" nature of abuse ranging from "insults and threats to physical assaults."[74] The ACLU report, co-written by the University of Chicago Law School's International Human Rights Clinic, says the U.S. government "failed to provide adequate safeguards and humane detention conditions for children in CBP custody." The report uses the word "sadistic." Some of the horrific treatment of immigrant children detailed aired on Public Radio.[75] NPR quoted the words of Mitra Ebadolahi, staff attorney with the ACLU's Border Litigation Project saying, "These documents provide a glimpse into a federal immigration enforcement system marked by brutality and lawlessness."[76] The time frame of the ACLU report may be surprising. This information was gathered between 2009 and 2014, during the Obama Administration, well before Trump came to office. Their treatment has only gotten worse under Trump.

On July 17, 2018, the *Huffington Post* reported on the findings of the Center for Human Rights and Constitutional Law, based on more than 200 accounts of migrant children and their parents. The report details sickening conditions and lack of medical care that children face in Border Patrol stations, ICE facilities, and detention centers. Over the course of four days in a Texas facility, a 16-year-old Honduran girl named Keylin was kicked by guards to keep her awake. She laid all night in fear on a cement floor, surrounded by chain-link. Keylin told lawyers that guards called the group of migrants "filthy" and made fun of them, and "female guards made girls' strip naked" before taking a shower, "so they could leer at their bodies."[77]

A team of over 100 lawyers compiled these, and many more equivalent testimonials, which exemplified roughly 90 percent of the stories collected. The lawyers spoke to children who were "crying, trembling, hungry, thirsty, sleepless, sick, and terrified." Executive director of the law center, Peter Schey, told the *Huffington Post*, "We see a policy of enforced hunger, enforced dehydration and enforced sleeplessness coupled with routine insults and physical assaults." He added, "The treatment of these children amounts to torture."[78]

In June 2018, Representative Jeff Merkley (D-OR) traveled to a facility in Brownsville Texas called Casa Padre, where 1,500 migrant children, boys between the age of 10 and 17, were being held. When he attempted to go inside authorities stopped him and said he didn't have permission to speak about the facility.[79] Journalists were allowed inside later that month, and one MSNBC reporter, Jacob Soboroff, described the former Walmart as a prison. He tweeted, "These kids are incarcerated."[80]

Though cameras were not allowed inside Casa Padre, Homeland Security released some images to journalists. One picture particularly, in stunning evidence of a culture of brutality and terror that is carried out in secrecy, and unacknowledged, with no countervailing force brought to bear that could spark a note of human decency. In a macabre display of cruelty, one image shows a mural inside the detention facility of a grinning Donald Trump. Next to the image is a quote printed in both English and Spanish that gloats: "Sometimes by losing a battle you find a new way to win the war."

Donald Trump, Demonization, and Electoral Politics

As we have seen, Trump was not the first one to tie criminality to migration, or to racialize U.S. immigration procedures, or to treat migrants in unspeakable ways. What Trump has done to accelerate the brutality is to foreground the attendant xenophobia, amplify it, and use it to mobilize racist and white supremacist elements in the United States, in order to win a presidential election. Bringing the politics of fear into mainstream political discourse, he manipulated and molded the language of dehumanization into campaign discourse, inserting it into mainstream sensibilities. By doing so, he not only rendered racist language more visible and recognizable, he solidified the politicization of migration and its criminalization. This combined with the perceived loss of white privilege, rendered immigrant demonization a classic scapegoating strategy. Now, electoral politics are deeply interwoven with militarism, security discourses, and anti-immigration that together have had major consequences for Border Patrol Policies and American democracy as well.

The Border Wall

If we now turn to the discourses of the border wall, we see that misinformation about migrant criminality has played a major role in further politicizing and militarizing the borderlands. False "facts" about the need for a wall, the details, costs, and mythic lexicon in general, have solidified security discourses.

Possibly the best discussion of the follies of a border wall, and the ever changing claims about the need for one, aired on HBO's *Last Week Tonight*, the comedy/news program hosted by John Oliver. In a little less than 20 minutes, Oliver exposes Trump's wide-ranging ramblings about a beautiful wall, including footage of an unhinged President holding up a boy in front of a mic to ask, "what will the wall be made of?"[81] Oliver shows clips of Trump at speeches where in increments, the cost of the wall goes from 4 billion, to 12 billion and on to over 22 billion dollars. Oliver then adds that the costs of maintenance will equal the cost of its building within 7 years. He shows how the wall creates areas where entire U.S. communities are positioned on its other side, in Mexico. He offers recent historical data that shows how the border fence already covers the frontier in many towns, how the government seized private land to build it, and how building the fence required the roll-back of environmental protections for endangered species, and other laws designed to protect conservation areas. Altogether, the wall becomes the fantasy of a mad president, railing at drug dealers and foreign criminals, who could just as easily dig under it, climb over it, jump down from it, and propel packages across it, as they do now.[82]

Trump's demand for a border wall has closed down the federal government and led to a state of emergency. But the consequences of militarization at the border, and the wall itself, are finally being scrutinized because of the escalating weaponizing of the border areas. Border policies are now being challenged by the communities who live in the borderlands.

Border towns have become a site of struggle in the United States. As these communities become *othered* by Trump, the responses from residents and local representatives have begun to crack the frames of security discourses. The 45th President's foregrounding of El Paso, Texas, illustrates these points.

The "Othering" of El Paso Texas

Hours before Trump was set to hold a campaign rally in El Paso, Texas, county officials there passed a resolution pushing back on the President's false claims. The resolution cites Trump's 2019 SOTU saying "El Paso was one of the most dangerous cities in the United States until the construction of border fencing," and goes on to point out that the claim was

> yet another lie that was quickly disputed by residents and members of our local law enforcement agencies. El Paso's violent crime rate dropped 62 percent from its peak in 1993 to 2007, a year before construction on the fence began.[83]

MSNBC correspondent Garrett Haake posted a photo of the resolution on twitter, with the caption "the county is disillusioned by President Trump's lies regarding the border and our community." News outlets such as CNN and *Newsweek* quoted from the resolution stating that Trump and his administration have "disseminated false information to local elected officials across the nation regarding its perceived need for border security funding priorities, including calling life on the U.S.-Mexico border a 'crisis situation.'" The resolution corrected such claims saying, "data from Customs and Border Protection (CBP) illustrates that no such crisis exists." The residents and the officials living in El Paso know well that Trump "has continuously made inaccurate claims about the United States' southern border." When these communities pushed back, their challenge opened media coverage to long overdue criticisms of security discourses.[84]

Escalating Militarization: Border Communities and the Wall

In a long article by the *Arizona Daily Star*, family-owned business-man Evan Kory is quoted, along with other residents of Nogales, Arizona: "You hear on the news that an invasion is coming, but in fact, border communities have been invaded by our own government." The article is titled, "Remove the Razor Wire, Some Arizona Residents Plead," and the headline is superimposed over a full-page visual of a fence covered with ominous-looking razor wire.[85] Two huge circles of wire hang on a border fence, dwarfing the landscape and the communities it separates. Before the caravan got to the United States, mainstream media covered troop movements being sent to confront the migrants, detailing the installation of wire along the southern border. In those stories media habitually referred to razor wire as *"concertina wire,"* a euphemistic term that calls forth such cultural references as music and dancing. But photographs of rows and rows of *razor wire* that now enclose border towns reveal the stunning realities of what it looks and feels like to live along a weaponized terrain. Another resident observed, "It looks like a war zone." Many interviews also provide information about the negative economic effects a militarization that have led to increased surveillance and long lines, which slow commerce on both sides where family-owned businesses once thrived.[86]

Prisoners of the Past, Victims of the Present

Whether it's ever built, that wall is already a symbol of a country in danger of walling itself in, psychologically speaking, and allowing its people to become what Grandin calls "prisoners of the past."[87] Other manifestations of the ways in which the United States is losing its once shinny gloss as a welcoming bastion of civil liberties, including freedom of speech, become more evident every day. One occurred at Trump's rally in El Paso, Texas, when a Trump supporter jumped onto the press platform and attacked a BBC journalist, responding to Trump's cries that the press are the enemy of the people.[88]

The people of the United States are now the victims of the continuing policies that have influenced and been influenced by border militarism and security discourses in general. Just ahead of the midterm elections, an outspoken supporter of President Trump was charged with sending at least a dozen pipe-bombs to prominent figures and politicians all of whom were regularly disparaged by Trump. Suspect Cesar Altieri Sayoc posted a picture of himself on social media wearing a Make America Great Again hat. He had been living out of a van in Florida, plastered with hateful images and slogans often repeated by the 45th President and also found on fringe right-wing social media sites.[89]

Alternet and the *Washington Post* reported on new research by University of North Texas political scientists Ayal Feinberg, Regina Branton, and Valerie Martinez-Ebers that offers additional evidence on the relationship between Donald Trump and racial violence in America. The authors examined the correlation between the counties that hosted one of Trump's 275 presidential campaign rallies in 2016 and increased incidents of hate crimes in subsequent months. "We found that counties that had hosted a 2016 Trump campaign rally saw a 226 percent increase in reported hate crimes over comparable counties that did not host such a rally."[90] A horrific incident that demonstrates the connections between Trump's rhetoric, the cultivation hatred and fear, and violent extremism, took place on October 27, 2018.[91] A shooter took the lives of 11 people in an episode of gun violence clearly inspired by the President's repeated demonization of immigrants as killers, rapists, and terrorists. The Tree of Life Synagogue had recently participated in the National Refugee Shabbat, a Jewish refugee resettlement agency in Pittsburgh. The gunman ranted against the refugee agency, claiming they were inviting "hostile invaders to dwell among us." Before killing 11 people in the Synagogue, the morning of the attack, Robert Bowers posted these words: "I can't sit by and watch my people get slaughtered….I'm going in."[92]

Conclusion

As violence increases along the border and in the detention facilities where migrants are held, the people of the United States have also become its victims, as the consequences of militarism follow a trajectory toward more violence and hatred. In so many ways, criminalization and militarization have led to a culture of violence in the Americas, and security discourses have contributed to the perpetuation of militarism for decades. Deep in the heartlands of America, people have become the targets of unhinged followers of a president willing to cynically manipulate fear to hold power. We will now turn to a discussion of steps that might be taken to break the cycle of violence, which causes so much pain and suffering across the hemisphere.

Notes

1 Francisco Cantu, "Has Any of Us Wept?" *New York Review of Books*, January 17, 2019, www.nybooks.com/articles/2019/01/17/has-any-one-of-us-wept/
2 Ibid., Cantu, 2019.
3 Office of Immigration Statistics, 2018, 13.
4 The same policy was engaged during the "migration" crisis in Europe when EU countries closed their borders and outsourced "security" to Turkey.
5 Leighton Akio Woodhouse, "Running for Their Lives: Fleeing Gangs, Central American Refugees Fight Deportation from the U.S.," *The Intercept*, May 18, 2016, https://theintercept.com/2016/05/18/fleeing-gangs-central-american-refugees-fight-deportation-from-the-u-s/
6 Dana Frank makes this point as well, noting that the scant media coverage of right-wing death squad murders in Honduras fell off the news agenda after the unaccompanied minors became the story.
7 Jake Johnston, "How Pentagon Official May Have Encouraged a 2009 Coup in Honduras," *The Intercept*, August 29, 2017, https://theintercept.com/2017/08/29/honduras-coup-us-defense-departmetnt-center-hemispheric-defense-studies-chds/
8 Ibid., Johnston, 2017
9 Ibid., Johnston, 2017.
10 Greg Grandin, *The Last Colonial Massacre*, Second Edition (Chicago, IL: University of Chicago Press, 2011).
11 Ibid., Grandin, 2011.
12 Ibid., Johnston, 2017.
13 Sarah Kinosian, "Crisis in Honduran Democracy has its Roots in U.S. Tacit Support for 2009 Coup," *The Guardian*, December 7, 2017, www.theguardian.com/world/2017/dec/07/crisis-of-honduras-democracy-has-roots-in-us-tacit-support-for-2009-coup
14 Ibid, Alex Emmons, 2016.
15 *Wall Street Journal*, "Green Berets Train Elite Police Units in Honduras," February 21, 2016, www.wsj.com/video/green-berets-train-elite-police-units-in-honduras/D80E3F64-F857-4439-892B-068B85445BBC.html
16 Daniel Beckman, "A Labyrinth of Deception: Secretary Clinton and the Honduran Coup," Council on Hemispheric Affairs, April 12, 2017, www.coha.org/a-labyrinth-of-deception-secretary-clinton-and-the-honduran-coup/#_edn7
17 Mr. Hernández was so established in trafficking, prosecutors said, that he had even had his own cocaine brand: Laboratories in Colombia and Honduras stamped packets with the initials T.H., for Tony Hernández. See Jeff Ernst and Elizabeth Malkin, *New York Times*, November 28, 2018, www.nytimes.com/2018/11/26/world/americas/honduras-brother-drug-charges.html
18 Ibid., Ernst and Malkin, 2018.
19 Mike LaSusa, "Former Honduras President's Son Pleads Guilty to US Drug Charges," InSight Crime, May 17, 2016, www.insightcrime.org/news-briefs/fmr-honduras-president-son-pleads-guilty-to-us-drug-charges

20 Ibid., Ernst and Malkin, 2018.
21 Ibid., Ernst and Malkin, 2018.
22 BBC News, "Honduran President's Brother Accused of Drug Trafficking," November 27, 2018, www.bbc.com/news/world-latin-america-46357509
23 Silvio Carrillo, "America's Blind Eye to Honduras's Tyrant," *New York Times*, December 19, 2017, www.nytimes.com/2017/12/19/opinion/america-honduras-hernandez-trump.html
24 Amnesty International, "Honduras: Government deploys dangerous and Illegal Tactics to Silence Population," December 8, 2017, www.amnesty.org/en/latest/news/2017/12/honduras-government-deploys-dangerous-and-illegal-tactics-to-silence-population/
25 Amnesty International, 2017.
26 Ibid., Carrillo, 2017.
27 *60 Minutes*, "The Chaos Behind Trump's Policy of Family Separation at the Border," CBS News, November 26, 2018, www.cbsnews.com/news/trump-family-separation-policy-mexican-border-60-minutes-investigation-greater-in-number-than-trump-administration-admits/
28 The United Nations and others in humanitarian affairs have come to call those not identified as refugees, "irregular migrants." These categories have been set in place in anticipation of an influx of migrations due to inevitable environmental catastrophes in the future.
29 Jemma M. Loyd and Alison Mountz, *Boats, Borders, and Bases: Race, the Cold War, and the Rise of Migration Detention in the United States* (Berkeley, CA: University of California Press, 2018).
30 Robin Andersen, "Reality TV and Criminal Injustice," *The Humanist* 54, no. 5 (September/October, 1994): 8–13, www.academia.edu/35001611/Reality_TV_and_Criminal_Injustice
31 Loyd and Mountz, 2018.
32 Greg Grandin and Elizabeth Oglesby, "Washington Trained Guatemala Killers for Decades," *The Nation*, January 25, 2019, www.thenation.com/article/border-patrol-guatemala-dictatorship/
33 Logan worked close to where the two Guatemalan children Jakelin Caal Maquín, and 8-year-old Felipe Gómez Alonzo, fell mortally ill in Border Patrol custody in December 2018. See Grandin and Elizabeth Oglesby, 2019.
34 Ibid., Grandin and Oglesby, 2019.
35 Ibid., Grandin and Oglesby, 2019.
36 Janine Jackson, "The Violence that Eliot Abrams supported is Unspeakable," Interview with Jon Swartz, *CounterSpin,* FAIR, March 6, 2019, https://fair.org/home/the-violence-elliott-abrams-supported-is-unspeakable/
37 Roxanne Lynborn Doty, "States of Exception on the Mexico–U.S. Border: Security, Decisions, and Civilian Border Patrols," *International Political Sociology* 1, no. 2 (2007): 113–37.
38 Cynthia Van Der Heyden, "Making the Minutemen: The Framing of the Minuteman Project in U.S. Television News," *Academia.org*, Bachelor's Thesis American Studies, 2014, www.academia.edu/8196663/Making_The_Minutemen._The_Framing_of_the_Minuteman_Project_in_U.S._Television_News

39 David Kelly, "Minutemen Prepare to Lay Down the Law," *Los Angeles Times*, April 2, 2005, http://articles.latimes.com/2005/apr/02/nation/na-minute2. Cited in Van Der Heyden 2014

40 Ibid., Kelly, 2005.

41 American Civil Liberties Union of Arizona, *Creating the Minutemen: A Small Extremist Group's Campaign Fueled by Misinformation* (New Mexico and Texas: ACLU of Arizona, 2006), www.ilw.com/articles/2006,0619-ybarra.pdf, accessed on April 4, 2014.

42 Leo Chavez, *The Latino Threat: Constructing Immigrants, Citizens, and the Nation* (California: Stanford University Press, 2008).

43 Michelle A. Holling, "Patrolling National Identity, Masking White Supremacy: The Minuteman Project," in *Critical Rhetorics of Race*. eds. Michael G. Lacy and Kent A. Ono (New York: New York University Press, 2011), 99

44 Ibid., Holling 2011, 99.

45 Joshua Grimm, "Patrolling Whiteness: Framing the Minuteman Project on the Evening News" (2008), The Annual Meeting of the International Communication Association in Montreal, http://citation.allacademic.com/meta/p_mla_apa_research_citation/2/3/3/2/2/pages233224/p233224-1.php

46 Ibid., Van Der Heyden 2014.

47 Ibid., Van Der Heyden 2014.

48 Associated Press, "Amid Concerns, Volunteer Border Patrol Grows," July 17, 2005. http://www.nbcnews.com/id/8607784/ns/us_news-life/t/amid-concerns-volunteer-border-patrol-grows/#.XIFBJNF7ld8

49 Ibid., Associated Press, 2005.

50 Though under pressure, commissioners insisted they were talking only about "illegal immigrants." Ibid., Associated Press, 2005.

51 Greg Grandin, "Bread, Circuses and Duct Tape," *TomDispatch.com*, March 5, 2019, www.tomdispatch.com/post/176535/tomgram%3A_greg_grandin%2C_donald_trump%2C_pornographer-in-chief/#more

52 YouTube, "1990 Fox's *The Reporters*," www.youtube.com/watch?v=FM609mv6BOw

53 The program is hosted by former *Newsday* investigative journalist Bob Drury, who tries to depict migrants sympathetically, but sympathy is outstripped by the sensationalized excitement of the chase scenes.

54 Grandin notes that "Drury linked this upsurge in border extremism to the end of the Vietnam War: many of the vigilantes were veterans of that war. Others were teenagers who modeled their tactics, including the setting of booby traps, on Vietnam War movies they had seen."

55 Ibid., Robin Andersen, 1994.

56 Militainment refers to the margining of the audio-visual environment with the ethos and strategies of military combat and battlefield priorities. Actively promoted by the Pentagon, film, television, and video games portray the Defense Forces in the best possible light, using state of the art weaponry and advanced military digital imagery. See Robin Andersen, *A Century of Media, A Century of War* (Peter Lang, 2006), and Roger Stahl, *Militainment, Inc.: War, Media and Popular Culture*, (Routledge, 2010)

57 Ibid., Greg Grandin, 2019.

58 YouTube, Border Wars—S02E04—Lost in the River www.youtube. com/watch?v=1ffu8c8Lnt8

59 Ibid., Greg Grandin, 2019.

60 Ibid., Greg Grandin, 2019.

61 Sarah Lynch Baldwin, "'Armed Vigilantes Illegally Detain Migrants' Near U.S.-Mexico Border, ACLU Says," CBS News, April 19, 2019.www. cbsnews.com/news/united-constitutional-patriots-aclu-says-armed-vigilantes-unlawfully-detaining-migrants-near-u-s-mexico-border/

62 Stephen Hopsgood, "Fascism Rising," *OpenGlobalRights*, November 9, 2016, www.openglobalrights.org/fascism-rising/

63 Katheryn Hampton, Zero Protection: "How U.S. Border Enforcement Harms Migrant Safety an Health," *Physicians for Human Rights*, January 10, 2019, https://phr.org/resources/zero-protection-how-u-s-border-enforcement-harms-migrant-safety-and-health/#top

64 Marilyn Haigh, "What's Happening at the Border: Here's What We Know About Immigrant Children and Family Separation," *The Texas Tribune*, June 18, 2018, www.texastribune.org/2018/06/18/separated-immigrant-children-families-border-mexico/

65 Ibid., Marilyn Haigh 2018. However, the *New York Times* reported that The Trump administration tested the "zero tolerance" policy starting in October. The *New York Times* reported, between October and April, more than 700 children were separated from adults. See Caitlin Dickerson, "Hundreds of Immigrant Children have been taken from Parents at U.S. Border," *New York Times*, April 20, 2018, www.nytimes. com/2018/04/20/us/immigrant-children-separation-ice.html

66 Ibid., Marilyn Haigh, 2018.

67 Roque Planas and Angelina Chapin, "California's Attorney General Says Immigration Should Be Decriminalized," *Huffington Post*, April 3, 2019, www.huffpost.com/entry/california-attorney-general-xavier-becerra-immigration-decriminalized_n_5ca38787e4b0c32979610abc?n-cid=newsltushpmgnews__TheMorningEmail__040419

68 Ed Lavandera, "She Says Federal Official Took Her Daughter While She Breastfed The Child in a Detention Center," CNN, June 14, 2018, www.cnn.com/2018/06/12/us/immigration-separated-children-southern-border/index.html

69 Ibid., Lavandera, 2018.

70 *Press From*, "Florida Detention Center Expands, Packing in Migrant Children 'Like Sardines,'" February 13, 2019, https://pressfrom.info/ us/news/us/-244598-florida-detention-center-expands-packing-in-migrant-children-like-sardines.html

71 Tara Francis Chan, "Migrant children say they've been forcibly drugged, handcuffed and abused in U.S. Government Detention,' *Business Insider*, June 21, 2018, www.businessinsider.com/migrant-children-forcibly-drugged-abused-in-us-government-detention-2018-6

72 A lawyer for her mother, Yazmin Juárez told NPR that "The medical care that Mariee received in Dilley was neglectful and substandard." He went on to describe conditions at Dilley as "unsanitary, unsafe and inappropriate for any small child." See Joel Rose, "A Toddler's Death Adds to Concerns About Migrant Detention," August 28, 2018, www. npr.org/2018/08/28/642738732/a-toddlers-death-adds-to-concerns-about-migrant-detention

73 ACLU, "Neglect and Abuse of Unaccompanied Immigrant Children by U.S. Customs and Border Protection," May 2018, www.dropbox. com/s/lplnnufjbwci0xn/CBP%20Report%20ACLU_IHRC%205.23%20 FINAL.pdf?dl=0

74 Richard Gonzales, "ACLU Report: Detained Migrant Children Subjected to Widespread abuse by officials," NPR, May 18, 2018, www.npr. org/sections/thetwo-way/2018/05/23/613907893/aclu-report-detained-immigrant-children-subjected-to-widespread-abuse-by-officia

75 One 16-year-old girl was forced to "spread her legs and [they] touched her private parts so hard that she screamed." In another example, staff "ran over a 17-year-old with a patrol vehicle and then punched him repeatedly." Ibid., Richard Gonzales, 2018.

76 Ibid., Richard Gonzales, 2018.

77 Angelina Chapin, "Drinking Toilet Water, Wide Spread Abuse: Report Details 'Torture' for Children Detainees," *Huffington Post*, July 17, 2018, www.huffingtonpost.com/entry/migrant-children-detail-experiences-border-patrol-stations-detention-centers_us_5b4d13ffe4b0de86f4 85ade8

78 Ibid., Angelina Chapin, 2018.

79 Ryan Bort, "This is the Prison-Like Border Facility Housing Migrant Children," *Rolling Stone*, June 14, 2018, www.rollingstone.com/politics/ politics-news/this-is-the-prison-like-border-facility-holding-migrant-children-628728/

80 Jacob Soboroff, "Serge in Children Separated at Border Floods Facility for Undocumented Immigrants," MSNBC, June 18, 2018.

81 HBO, "Border Wall: Last Week Tonight with John Oliver," March 20, 2016, www.youtube.com/watch?v=vU8dCYocuyI

82 *ProPublic* has done a number of powerful stories of child separation at the border, and revealing stories about the realities of the wall. See for example, T. Christian Miller, "If Trump's Border Wall Becomes Reality, Here's How He Could Easily Get Private Land for It," March 25, 2019, www.propublica.org/article/if-trumps-border-wall-becomes-reality-heres-how-he-could-easily-get-private-land-for-it

83 Laura Clawson, "El Paso County Commission Minces No Words, Calls Out Trumps' Lies on Border Walls and Crime," *Daily Kos*, February 11, 2019, www.dailykos.com/stories/2019/2/11/1833944/-El-Paso-county-commission-minces-no-words-calls-out-Trump-s-lies-about-border-walls-and-crime

84 The Hill https://thehill.com/blogs/blog-briefing-room/news/429476-el-paso-county-passes-resolution-that-it-is-disillusioned-by

85 Perla Traviso, "Remove the Razor Wire, Some Arizona Residents Plead," *Arizona Daily Star*, February 26, 2019, https://tucson.com/news/local/remove-the-razor-wire-some-arizona-border-town-residents-plead/article_bfcdd35e-5f33-59a4-9f69-9893e3e49b3f.html

86 Ibid., Perla Traviso, 2019.

87 Tomgram, "Greg Grandin, Donald Trump, Pornographer-in-Chief," *TomDispatch.com*, March 5, 2019, www.tomdispatch.com/post/176535/ tomgram%3A_greg_grandin%2C_donald_trump%2C_pornographer-in-chief/#more

88 Jen Hayden, "Trump Supporter Jumped onto Media Platform and Attacked a BBC Cameraman at MAGA Rally," *Daily Kos*, February 12,

2019, www.dailykos.com/stories/2019/2/12/1834127/-Trump-supporter-jumped-onto-media-platform-and-attacked-a-BBC-cameraman-at-MAGA-rally?detail=emaildkre

89 William K. Rashbaum, Alan Feuer, and Adam Goldman, "Outspoken Trump Supporter in Florida Charges with attempted bombing Spree," *New York Times*, October 26, 2018, www.nytimes.com/2018/10/26/ny region/cnn-cory-booker-pipe-bombs-sent.html

90 Chauncey DeVega, "Donald Trump and Racist Violence: Research points to a Clear Connection," *Alternet*, March 31, 2019, www.alternet.org/2019/03/donald-trump-and-racist-violence-research-points-to-a-clear-connection/

91 For a discussion of how hate speech cultivates hated, and leads to extreme violence, even genocide, See, Adama Dieng and Simona Cruciani, "When Media is Used to Incite Violence: The United Nations, Genocide and Atrocity Crimes," in *The Routledge Companion to Media and Humanitarian Action*, ed. Robin Andersen and Purnaka L. de Silva (New York: Routledge, 2018).

92 Ashley Murray, "Pittsburgh's Jewish Refugee Resettlement Agency, HIAS Vow to Continue Work after Threats, Squirrel Hill Shooting," *Pittsburgh Post-Gazette*, October 30, 2018, www.post-gazette.com/local/city/2018/10/30/Pittsburgh-jewish-refugee-resettlement-HIAS-squirrel-hill-synagogue-shooting/stories/201810300100

Coda
Solutions—Changing Course, Discourse, and Media Frames

Robin Andersen

Coda

How do we begin to reverse the cycles of violence discussed in this volume, and the seemingly unstoppable movement toward more security, brutality, and militarism? How do we begin to right the wrongs done to the innocent, and set a course aimed at peace and stability, shared humanity and cultures, and true human equality? How can we start to build hemispheric prosperity and stop the destructive forces pushing us toward poverty and death? Space does not allow us here to answer these questions in the depth and complexity they deserve. But we will begin this discussion, and offer some alternative ways of thinking and speaking about the problems of forced migrations, (and immigration in general) and the histories that lie hidden under the visible surfaces of those who suffer.

Looking Away from the Enduring Allure of Security Discourses

Currently, no real challenges exist to abolish, or even reform the "border protection" system. Even in the face of documentation and evidence of an enduring culture of cruelty and militarism, deeply entrenched practices of Border Agencies persist. Writing for *Foreign Policy in Focus* Khury Petersen-Smith identified how "security" continues to dominate political dialogue in the United States. He recognizes that in debates between the White House and Capitol Hill, the "question has been not *whether* to militarize the border, but merely how many billions of dollars should be devoted to 'border security,' or what specific physical infrastructure it should buy."[1] He also observes that a *genuine* call for open borders is virtually nonexistent.

Underscoring these observations was the official democratic reply by Stacey Abrams to Trump's State of the Union address in January 2019. Her words were framed by security discourses when she promised that "Democrats stand ready to effectively secure our ports and borders." Indeed, she saw no contradiction between a call for humanitarian principles and border security, when she announced "compassionate treatment is not the same as open borders." Yet in the long historical movement to militarism through brutality and on to the torture of children, the road to security and the one to compassion have traveled in different directions for decades. As we have argued in these pages, they will never arrive at the same destination. Like the image of a grinning Donald Trump tormenting the incarcerated children he has subjugated, compared to the photograph of the migrant mother running from tear-gas holding fast to her girls—one boldly celebrates the brutality of Empire, and the other evokes outrage at the inhumanity of Empire's practices. One shakes a fist at refugees, the other wonders why they are not welcome. They represent divergent human sensibilities; on the one hand, an uncaring culture of Empire, the other exposing it. How do we move toward a culture that can empathize with the common struggles of global humanity and offer a welcoming embrace?

The Call for Open Borders

Khury Petersen-Smith argues that the time has come to call for open borders, and that the politics of open borders can win over the electorate. But what would the call for open borders actually demand? How would we lay the foundation for such dramatic discursive and policy shifts?

An Apology to the People of Central America

To launch a bold trajectory aimed at breaking the constraints of security discourses, the next President of the United States might begin with an apology, a sincere regret spoken at the site of a massacre or protest where peaceful people were murdered in Central America. Journalist and writer Raymond Bonner launched this idea in 2016 when he wrote, "Obama recently expressed regret for US support of Argentina's 'dirty war.' It's time Washington did the same regarding our active backing of right-wing butchery in El Salvador."[2] A Presidential admission should be covered with the attendant media attention it would deserve, attention equivalent to say, the Royal Wedding, which garnered triple the media coverage of Yemen in 2018.[3] As Ray Bonner the journalist who documented the El Mozote Massacre observed, an apology to the people of El Salvador would openly recognize and take responsibility for the loss of life and destruction that took place in that country throughout the 1980s. Speaking about Argentina, Obama admitted, "We've been slow to speak out for human rights and that was the case here."[4] Indeed that has been the case in Central America for decades. Accepting responsibility would also be extended to the U.S. backing of the coup in Honduras and the death, violence, and environmental degradation that has befallen the people there since 2009. In Guatemala, the acknowledgement would have to extend even further back historically, and then especially to the genocide of the Mayan people carried out by General Efraín Ríos Montt, who received words of praise and support from Ronald Reagan. This proposal may begin to sound ridiculous, even facetious, but it is not. Admittedly, it would be a dramatic departure from the way the current U.S. President characterizes El Salvador as a "shithole" country.[5] But the idea that it sounds impossible for a U.S. head of state to tell the truth is what should amaze us. Such an announcement would begin to crack security discourses in ways that might easily shatter the frame to pieces. As news media began to make sense of the apology, they would have to look back historically and recount the history of U.S. wars in the hemisphere. Such reporting might begin to explain why the countries of the Northern Triangle have become uninhabitable for so many of its people.

In Argentina, President Obama praised two American diplomats, Tex Harris and Patt Derian, for their commitment to documenting the human-rights abuses in Argentina. Bonner argues that a junior diplomat in the U.S. embassy, H. Carl Gettinger, should in like manner, be recognized for his work in El Salvador. It was Gettinger who enlisted a Salvadoran army lieutenant to help him solve the case of the four churchwomen who were raped and murdered in El Salvador in late 1980. The lieutenant had so much blood on his hands that Gettinger dubbed him the "killer," but he gave Gettinger, and the United States, the name of the sergeant who led the operation to kill the women. Gettinger risked his career and his life to carry out his own investigation after Washington slandered the women and ignored the killings. In 1984, the sergeant and four other soldiers were convicted of the crime that senior Salvadoran military commanders had successfully covered up until then.[6]

Acknowledging the El Mozote Massacre

In a 2016 tribute to the people of El Salvador that recounts the El Mozote Massacre, the authors conclude with this thought:

> El Mozote showed what the Salvadoran regime was capable of, and what the US government was willing to tolerate, excuse, and cover for in service of supposed anticommunism.
>
> After it became clear that the Atlacatl battalion had decapitated men in a church and bayoneted a child to death and slaughtered entire families, the obvious questions for the Reagan administration were: are these crimes barbaric enough to convince you to change course? Is there any limit to the kind of vile acts you will excuse in order to pursue your foreign policy aims?
>
> The answer to both questions, provided by El Mozote and its aftermath: a resounding "no."[7]

Recognition for those who advocate to put an end to violence is a precedent that has been set by a number of other institutions.

Recognizing and Honoring those Who Fight for Human Rights

American media heroes are most often depicted as soldiers and combatants—those who have medals pinned on their uniforms followed by a salute. Those who fight for justice through peaceful means, using human rights law, investigations, and accountability remain the unsung heroes on the margins of media culture. At the University of Dayton, the Romero Human Rights Award for 2019 will be given to three individuals who investigated the El Mozote Massacre.[8] This announcement was met with little media attention, but the *National Catholic Reporter* listed David Morales as an honoree.[9] Morales formerly served as the human rights ombudsman for the Salvadoran government, now heads the Cristosal's Observatory on Forced Displacement by Violence covering El Salvador, Guatemala, and Honduras. Cristosal's mission is to promote human rights in Central America through "rights-based research, learning, and programming." Ovidio Mauricio Gonzalez and Wilfredo Medrano who have worked with Tutela Legal, a human rights agency that collected evidence of abuse during El Salvador's civil war from 1979 to 1992. In November 1991, Tutela Legal published the first comprehensive investigation of El Mozote and recorded 794 names of those murdered. The agency continues to focus on issues of state violence, promoting justice and accountability.

Saint Óscar Romero

The Romero Human Rights Award is named after Óscar Arnulfo Romero, the Archbishop of San Salvador who was assassinated by a right-wing death squad in 1980. In 2015, Pope Francis declared that Archbishop died a martyr.[10] Then on October 14, 2018, the Pope canonized the late Salvadoran archbishop, who was shot as he celebrated mass in a hospital chapel. He will henceforth be known as Saint Óscar Romero. *The New Yorker* reported that the canonization ceremony was streamed live on giant video screens in the plaza outside the main cathedral in the capital city of San Salvador where Romero is interred. As discussed in Chapter 1, Romero's funeral had been held in that same plaza where army snipers and death-squad gunmen killed at least 42 people and wounded 200 more.[11] Writer Jon Lee Anderson acknowledges his mixed feeling attending the canonization because the Archbishop's killers have never been held accountable, even though Roberto d'Aubuisson is widely known to have organized Romero's assassination. Anderson laments, "infuriating was the sight of Alfredo Cristiani, who had signed the amnesty that prevented Romero's killers being held to account, and d'Aubuisson's namesake son, an *ARENA* politician, seated in the V.I.P. section."[12]

The Economics of "Border Security"

At a congressional hearing held on January 29, 2019, Department of Defense officials projected the cost of the deployment of the National Guard across the U.S.-Mexico border to be $550 million through fiscal year 2019.[13] Another $132 million had already been spent on active-duty military securing the border, and officials could not estimate the cost for the rest of the fiscal-year. Then on March 10, 2019, news media reported that Donald Trump's proposed budget for the year 2020 allocated 8.6 billion dollars to the border wall. Media outlets featured glaring headlines about the 8.6 billion dollar allocation. The *Washington Post* focused on how the battle for wall funding would play out between the executive and legislative branches.[14] Others, especially alternative media, also viewed Trump's budget critically, observing that it increased the deficit, delivered more wealth to the wealthy, expanded an already bloated military budget, and made deep cuts in the social safety net. *Alternet* ran a headline quoting Bernie Sanders calling it "breathtaking in its degree of cruelty."[15] Trump's budget would also slash funding for science, medicine, and the environment.[16] Many media narratives presented border wall funding as an exciting government fight, one that might lead to another crisis. Missed was the opportunity to explore the connections between funding a wall and the actual crisis in Central America that causes out-migration. Not one media outlet pointed out that if a fraction of the billions of dollars allocated for the militarization of the border, and a wall, were to be spent on immediate humanitarian aid and to bolster democratic institutions, and rebuild local economies in the countries of the Northern Triangle, forced migrations could be a thing of the past.

A Real "Marshall Plan"

In a few policy circles, the idea for a new Marshall Plan for the region is currently more than a whisper. As an alternative to U.S. military policy in the region, a real Marshall Plan could help set the region on a new course. U.S. policy and aid to Central America has been rewarding brutal military governments in the Northern Triangle for years. But new funding, and an increase in aid, would have to be allocated in ways that directly benefit those in need, beginning with the largely unrecognized population of Internally Displaced Persons. Other, more long-term development plans would build the civilian economy in ways not designed to benefit global investment markets, or multinational corporate interests such as bio-fuels that push indigenous peoples off their land. Market-based solutions to poverty have been the preferred strategies in the era of neoliberal globalization, and are taken for granted as legitimate development practices in media, but market-based solutions financed by international lending have only exacerbated global poverty.[17]

Instead, programs and infrastructure would have to be built through partnerships with local grass-roots organizations, environmental and human rights organizers, international development bodies, and activists who can help build anti-poverty social programs, restore gender equality and democratic institutions. Funding should be made available to compile documentation that could lead to the dismantling of paramilitary forces in the service of multinational corporate interests, and that are involved in the drug trade.

Halting State Sponsored Murder and Demanding Accountability

Continuing to justify military funding for repressive regimes by invoking the war on drug makes no sense as elements within the governments of the Northern Triangle have all been involved with the drug cartels. After another illegitimate election took place in Honduras on November 26, 2017, Amnesty International offered a first-step strategy: "Halting all use of illegitimate or excessive force against protesters by security forces, ending arbitrary detentions, and investigating all instances of human rights violations would be a good start to undo some of the many wrongs we have documented."[18] Prosecutions and sanctions for those responsible for continuing human rights abuses would quickly result in a change of course. Justice would be served, and as many who understand the essential interrelationship between peace and justice, the need for justice is essential to peace. The activists, family members, and lawyers who worked to bring General Efraín Ríos Montt to justice in Guatemala understood this relationship. Writing about the trial in an article titled, "Impunity's Eclipse," the author concludes by explaining the Mayan concept of justice, which is called "labenxe," meaning "change." Those involved in the Ríos Montt Tribunal understood that, in a country wracked by violence and brutality, change is what is needed. And that change will lead to "living in peace. Because if there is no justice, there is no peace. If there is no justice, impunity continues to exist. The crimes they committed may be repeated."[19]

Stop the Growth of Detention Centers and the Brutality Against Migrants

Halting the growth of a new migrant-detention industrial complex is essential at this time. Once corporate profits are allocated to lobby government representatives, momentum for more detention infrastructure will build in the United States. In this regard, the American Friends Service Committee has had an enormous success. On March 5, 2019, Caliburn International, a for-profit company that runs the Homestead detention center incarcerating migrant children in Florida, cancelled its planned stock offering— to sell $100 million in shares. The company cited "market forces." The announcement came amid public outcry over the company's profiting from locking up children. As the AFSC rightly boasted,

"It seems that attention from the media, activists, and others is making an impact!" As the largest detention site for migrant children in the United States, and an "emergency" facility, it is exempt from many federal laws and regulations. As we detailed in Chapter 5, in facilities like these children can languish for months. AFSC staff and constituents spoke at press conferences, and through a well-designed national campaign, the *Miami Herald* covered the protest, airing a videotape that told the story, and demonstrated outspoken public opposition to for-profit detention facilities.[20]

In addition, the *Washington Post* reported on March 3, 2019, that JPMorgan Chase, the nation's largest bank, became "the latest major corporation to distance itself from Trump's immigration policies, concluding that its investments in private detention centers conflicted with its broader business strategy."[21] Over the course of a two-year campaign, protesters disrupted shareholder meetings, delivered petitions imploring the bank to "break up with private prison companies," and blasted the recorded cries of separated immigrant children begging for their parents. They brought a mariachi band to the Manhattan apartment of JPMorgan Chase's chief executive Jamie Dimon. Wells Fargo and U.S. Bank will soon divest from for-profit prisons. Coverage by mainstream media outlets of such democratic actions in the face of unpopular government policies marks a significant moment for the possibility of social change.

Halt Military and Executive Branch Violations of First Amendment Rights at the Border

The historical interrelationships between militarism, domestic surveillance, and media censorship have been well documented.[22] Challenges to democratic institutions and freedom of speech go hand-in-hand with a growing military industrial complex, of the kind we are seeing in the borderlands of the United States. These interconnections have become evident in the practices of law enforcement and military deployments at the border. Journalists, especially those working free-lance, who covered the migrant caravan have become targets of surveillance by law enforcement agencies. The NBC affiliate NBC7 in San Diego published leaked documents from an anonymous source at the Department for Homeland Security in San Diego. Dated January 9, 2019, the document is titled, "San Diego Sector Foreign Operations Branch: Migrant Caravan FY-2019, Suspected Organizers, Coordinators, Instigators and Media," and details a surveillance program called "Operation

Secure Line."[23] A database of faces contained in small squares is pictured, in mug shot style, of activists and reporters working at the border. In addition, free-lance journalists report being repeatedly stopped at the border, detained, and questioned, asked for names of organizers, and if they recognized photographs of other people under surveillance.[24] In an acknowledgement of the dangers of such practices, a senior ICE official not involved in the surveillance told BuzzFeed News, "it is hard to support this activity."[25]

Journalists and legal advocacy organizations were less reserved in their outrage at the clear violations of the First Amendment. American Civil Liberties Union attorney Esha Bhandari, said in a statement to NBC7. "The government cannot use the pretext of the border to target activists critical of its policies, lawyers providing legal representation, or journalists simply doing their jobs."[26] And Sue Udry, executive director of Defending Rights and Dissent said. "The U.S. border has become a Constitution-free zone, and CBP is an agency out of control." She added, rightly, that it was time for Congress to step in.

Context and Background Must be Considered
Professional Mandates of Journalism

For the media's part, they must stop presenting the public with news from nowhere. We have made that argument throughout these pages; the public can only understand the causes of forced-migrations from the Northern Triangle if the history of militarization is told. Memory and history are intertwined in narrative constructions. There are many examples of how the lack of historical reporting continues to propel military adventures into the future. Missed opportunities to incorporate background and context abound in a world of failed wars and military growth, particularly with the appointment of government officials such as John Kelly.

Who is John Kelly?

When John Kelly became Donald Trump's White House Chief of Staff, he was widely anointed by the press as "the adult in the room." Kelly's "adult" moniker first emerged in a private email written by Ty Cobb, the White House Council, who referred to himself and Kelly as the adults in the room, to justify his involvement in the Trump Administration.[27] When challenged, Cobb replied "more adults in the room will be better. Me and Kelly among others."

After that, Kelly's image was carefully cultivated in media with few exceptions.[28] Media were so accepting of the former General that his pronouncements about child separation at the border are left unchallenged. In an interview with NPR, when asked if it would be "cruel and heartless" to separate a mother from her children at the border, Kelly responded, "I wouldn't put it quite that way. The children will be taken care of—**put into foster care or whatever.**" [Emphasis added] And he goes on, "But the big point is they elected to come illegally into the United States, and this is a technique that no one hopes will be used extensively or for very long."[29]

Here the interview ends with no follow-up question. Kelly is given the last word, allowed to deflect any notion of compassion and deflect the brutality of a "zero tolerance" policy. In light of such uncritical media, Kelly was allowed to disavow any personal responsibility for the child separation policy, and after resigning as Chief of Staff, he went on to deny that he had anything to do with it. He claimed to be surprised when he heard Jeff Sessions's announcement of the program.[30]

But for years Kelly's influence on current policy on Central America has been significant. Before becoming White House chief of staff, Kelly was Trump's pick for Secretary at the Department of Homeland Security, which helps design immigration policies. But retired General John Kelly's most important role was before that, as the head of SOUTHCOM, the Pentagon's Latin American subsidiary, the U.S. Southern Command from 2012 to 2016. As documented by Jake Johnston, SOUTHCOM was deeply involved in backing the illegal military coup in Honduras in 2009.[31] Indeed, when SOUTHCOM's mission moved from fighting communism to the War on Drugs in the 1990s, SOUTHCOM's budget increased "more than any other U.S. military regional command." At SOUTHCOM John Kelly was "one of the most vocal proponents of extending the U.S.'s Global War on Terrorism to Latin America." Johnston asserts, "nothing raises money in Congress quite like the supposed threats of drugs, radical leftism, and migrants." Kelly has had a close relationship with the current Honduran dictator, and has referred to Juan Orlando Hernández, as a "great guy" and a "good friend."[32]

Given the role Kelly has played in militarizing U.S. policies in Central America and undoubtedly, his words in a recent interview are all the more stunning. He said, "Illegal immigration into the

U.S. will only subside when our country's "demand for drugs" decreases and economic opportunity in Central America increases."[33] For a man whose military life has been devoted to the hemispheric "war and drugs," at the expense of the lives and livelihoods of the peoples of the Americas, it's a stunning set of pronouncement that can only be made in a media environment where they are received with little more than a sigh.

Elliott Abrams: From El Salvador to Venezuela

Much the same can be said for the long, storied past of Donald Trump's current Special Envoy to Venezuela, Elliott Abrams. When Archbishop Romero was assassinated in 1980, within eight months a military informant gave the U.S. embassy in El Salvador evidence that it had been plotted by Roberto D'Aubuisson. Ray Bonner offers details of this, referring to a CIA report to the White House at the time, of how D'Aubuisson, the leader of an ultra-right wing paramilitary death squad, had presided over a meeting in which soldiers drew lots for the right to kill the archbishop.[34] Yet, Elliott Abrams, working for the State Department in Central America during the Reagan administration, continued to welcome D'Aubuisson to the U.S. embassy in El Salvador. Abrams testified before Congress that he would not consider D'Aubuisson an extremist. "You would have to be engaged in murder."[35] But as Bonner concludes, "D'Aubuisson *was* engaged in murder, and Washington knew it." Elliot Abrams was also instrumental in covering up the El Mozote Massacre. He discredited the journalists who documented it, and ensured that the war would continue by certifying that the Salvadoran military was not violating human rights.[36]

Elliott Abrams would go on to be convicted in 1991 of misleading Congress about the shipment of arms to the anti-Sandinista forces in Nicaragua, in the Iran/Contra affair. He was pardoned by President George H.W. Bush, and later served as special adviser to President George W. Bush, ironically, on the issues of democracy and human rights. Today Abrams is working hard to foment a regime change in Venezuela, which would reprise the failed policies detailed in these pages. As this book goes to print, municipalities and grass-roots campaigners are actively working to stop such a reckless plan.

For example, at a recent monthly meeting, the San Francisco Democratic County Central Committee adopted a resolution on

Venezuela opposing "any military intervention in Venezuela; all covert interference in that nation's affairs; the use of economic sanctions and assets seizures designed to further immiserate its people; and all further measures designed to impose so-called 'regime change' from Washington."[37] This resolution is at odds with California's Democratic Congresswoman, Nancy Pelosi and current Speaker of the House of Representative, who like Donald Trump, explicitly endorsed the call for regime change.[38] As *Common Dreams* argues, traditionally, foreign military adventures have not been a matter of great domestic concern, but that could be changing. When a group of military veterans launched its "End the Forever War" campaign, they secured the support of Senators Bernie Sanders and Elizabeth Warren. The two pledged to "fight to reclaim Congress's constitutional authority to conduct oversight of U.S. foreign policy and independently debate whether to authorize each new use of military force, and act to bring the Forever War to a responsible and expedient conclusion."[39] On an optimistic note, Gallagher concludes that, a rise in the awareness of the disastrous nature of our foreign policy may now seem inevitable.[40]

International Coalitions and Partnerships: We are Fighting the Same Battles

In a 2017 report titled, "Defenders of the Earth", *Global Witness* documented the murder of 200 killings across 24 countries, compared to 185 across 16 in 2015. Almost 40 percent of those murdered were indigenous. The report notes that it has never been deadlier to take "a stand against companies that steal land and destroy the environment." Nearly four people were murdered every week in 2016 protecting their land and the natural world from industries like mining, logging, and agribusiness.[41] Today, especially in Honduras and Guatemala, native communities fight the extractive industries, with multinationals enlisting corrupt military and para-military security forces to kill environmental activists and push people off their lands. These are the same battles waged by environmentalists to save the earth across the global, particularly in the United States as Trump denies climate change, dismantles the EPA, and continues to support development of the worst of the extractive industries. As the environmental public sphere follows the lead of *Global Witness* and other cross-border organizations, they will help shine a spotlight on the murders of indigenous environmental defenders killed on the front lines of the environmental battle.

Overall, increasingly under the regime of the 45th president, U.S. citizens are fighting the same battles against the criminalization of protest, and greater inequality in the United States, the struggles for health care and social security, education, gender, and racial equality. Fighting for human rights in the face of police brutality are all part of a sweeping agenda taking hold across the globe. These struggles have been brutally repressed in the countries of the Northern Triangle. Activists organizations, international bodies and NGO's are helping shine a light on these global struggles and incorporating them into their advocacy campaigns, actions that are essential for reversing planetary destruction and the attendant humanitarian crises it will bring about.

Challenging the Pro-Military Bias of the Media

In a scathing email sent out widely to news outlets announcing his resignation, one journalist condemned what he identified as a pro-military bias in the U.S. media. The NBC/MSNBC reporter, William Arkin, a prominent war and military reporter, said he was leaving the network because of its "superficial and reactionary coverage of national security."[42] He charged news media with being "reflexively pro-war" and serving as a "prime propaganda instrument of the War Machine's promotion of militarism." As a result of NBC/MSNBC's all-consuming militarism, he said, the national security establishment has gained dangerous strength and "is ever more autonomous and practically impervious to criticism."[43] He claimed that news media has sacrificed "all journalistic standards and skepticism about generals and the U.S war machine."[44] These words are harsh and uncompromising in their criticism, but they nevertheless resonate with a prominent and growing body of literature by researchers, scholars, and news-watch organizations that make similar points, and warn that the merger between the media industries with the military industrial complex has led to the failure of U.S. corporate media to scrutinize the military, or criticize its often hidden operations.[45] Films and television narratives routinely celebrate the military, its personnel and weaponry, and the national security state.[46] Media has become a willing player when successive presidents call for war. Throughout the pages of this book, we have seen that over decades, media have gotten the story of war in Central America wrong, either through omission and framing, or through fear and favor. Media encouraged anti-immigrant sentiments along the border through TV reality shows, and they routinely adopt discursive security frames. There is little resistance to, or alternative narratives that might counter the logics of security, and so militarism moves forward. But we have also seen that cracks have begun to shake the dominant news framing, and pubic challenges grow to the uncritical acceptance of further military adventures. In addition, there is important push-back to the excessive militarization at the Southwestern borderlands. All of these are hopeful signs for a movement away from brutality and conflict and toward peace and stability. There are alternatives to the promotion of endless conflict. As the world stands on the brink of ever more dangerous and destructive conflict, and even nuclear war, a peace perspective should be the default position, and a starting point when covering belligerencies.

Changing the Frame from Security and Militarism to Peaceful Negotiation, Compassion, and Prosperity

In Chapter 2, we outlined the negotiated settlement reached between gangs and the government of El Salvador that led to the dramatic decrease in death and violence. The truce achieved in El Salvador demonstrated that there is a pathway to negotiating an end to violence. The truce was derailed as a new presidential election drew near, and contending political parties found it easier to revert back to an identifiable enemy for their own political needs. The demonization of enemies has long served the needs of politicians and despots, and such rhetoric is certainly not new. But without a discursive framework for peace, and lacking the language of human rights and humanitarian sensibilities of compassion and empathy, such language is nurtured and able to reach its full destructive force.

Demonization comes in many forms. Take for example the words of John Kelly in the NPR interview, as he laid the groundwork for justifying the zero tolerance policies at the border. Speaking about Central American migrants Kelly said, "They don't speak English, obviously that's a big thing. They don't speak English. They don't integrate well, they don't have skills."[47] These words should reveal to any careful listener, that Kelly is "othering" the people of Central America, only using slightly more refined language. He is arguing that they should not enter the country because they are not like us, and that we need to protect ourselves from them because they are somehow inferior to us. In fact, as we have seen with those who organize to keep their land in the face brutal military evictions and attacks, they are actually just like us, and forced to be brave and determined. Importantly, this language also ignores decades of humanitarian principles that recognizes universal human equality and dignity, the underpinnings of giving care and aid to those who are persecuted. A journalism frame that starts from a humanitarian perspective can alter discourses that demonize, and recognize such falsities for what they are.

Economic Arguments and Open Borders

John Kelly's assertion that Central American immigrants "don't integrate well, they don't have skills" implies that immigrants will be unsuccessful and therefore a burden to the economy. But that argument is easily dispensed with, belied by a spate of economic data demonstrating the opposite. As immigration expert and writer Brianna Rennix points out, "One 2014 economic Policy Institute Analysis found that immigrants, though 33% of the population, accounted for 15% of economic productivity."[48] In terms of economic impact, Rennix says the only other main economic argument is "immigrants will flood the labor market and compete for jobs with citizen workers particularly those in low-wage jobs." In her piece titled, "What Democrats Get Wrong About Immigration," Rennix challenges these assertion and advises Democrats to reframe this debate, reject the premise, and turn it around. She argues immigration is not the problem:

> The hoarding of resources by the comfortable and greedy in the US and around the world is the problem. The left should not merely seek to reform our immigration bureaucracy. We should seek to abolish the components of a system that is designed to police and punish the poor and working-class, and focus our energies on our real opponents.[49]

Indeed, labor unions have already contested the discourse that frames immigrants as competition for low-wage jobs. In recent years, the AFL-CIO released a "tool kit" for unions that outlines the ways to combat workplace ICE raids and fight "the narrative that immigrants 'take jobs.'"[50] In 2017 the AFL-CIO immigration policy stated that

> Pitting worker against worker is an age-old tactic of the boss to distract us from the real issues, divide us and keep us poor—and

we will not fall for it. The only way to stop the race to the bottom in wages and standards is for working people of all races, religions and immigration status to stand together and demand that corporate power be put in check. This will be done not by deporting immigrants and scapegoating them for the precarious labor market.[51]

Given these realities, Rennix also calls on Democratic to put forth proposals for open borders. This call is supported by polling data that demonstrates "a quite astonishingly progressive impulse on emigration (and taxes) within the body politic," particularly after the 2018 midterm elections. Candidates like Kansas Republican Kris Kobach, who embraced Trump's anti-immigration message in the 2018 midterms, "resoundingly lost, and a study of the swing states of Colorado and Pennsylvania found that anti-immigrant campaign rhetoric backfired."[52] When the U.S. public saw pictures of the brutality against immigrants at the border, Trump's caravan invasion scare also backfired. After the caravan, a gallop poll found that 81 percent of respondents supported a path to legalization.

Media texts are powerful indications of the way history will be remembered and understood. As the first draft of history, news texts and visual language help shape our collective memories. We also know that what is left undocumented, unexplained, and omitted also shape the way present policies are formulated and understood. U.S. media and the public have lost the background needed to understand present government policies, especially the knowledge that could connect the present crisis of brutality toward immigrants, to the long history of U.S. wars in the hemisphere. Trump's immigration crisis is a manufactured political crisis, not a real one. Countervailing forces in our own government must begin to challenge Trump's justifications, discourse, and policies, and not acquiesce to security discourses. Central American refugees must be treated with the dignity and compassion that humanity demands. We have seen, when media report the consequences of the brutality of militarism, festering, and now challenged along the southwestern borderlands, the public responds with compassion and outrage. If media provided a framework able to foreground the needs of the peoples of the Americas, including those in the United States, instead of the militarized, political demands for security, themes of compassion and empathy could begin to define a new world of peace and prosperity.

Notes

1 Khury Petersen-Smith, "Progressive Should Support Open Borders – With no Apology," *Foreign Policy in Focus*, February 21, 2019, https://fpif.org/progressives-should-support-open-borders-with-no-apology/
2 Raymond Bonner, "Time for a U.S. Apology to El Salvador," *New York Times*, April 15, 2016, www.thenation.com/article/time-for-a-us-apology-to-el-salvador/
3 This figure comes from the annual content analysis of media topics published by the authoritative Tyndall Report. See Jim Lobe, "Royal Wedding got triple the Media Coverage of Yemen in 2018," *Consortium News*, March 7, 2019.
4 Ibid., Raymond Bonner, 2016.
5 Raymond Bonner, "America's Role in El Salvador's Deterioration," *The Atlantic*, January 20, 2018, www.theatlantic.com/international/archive/2018/01/trump-and-el-salvador/550955/
6 Ibid., Raymond Bonner, 2016.
7 Micah Uetricht and Branko Marcetic, "Remember El Mozote," *Jacobin Magazine*, December 12, 2016, https://jacobinmag.com/2016/12/el-mozote-el-salvador-war-reagan-atlacatl-massacre
8 University of Dayton, "University of Dayton to Honor Human Rights Activists for Investigating, Prosecuting State-Sponsored Killings in Latin America," Press Release, March 15, 2019, www.udayton.edu/news/articles/2019/03/romero_award.php
9 Maria Benevento, "El Mozote Massacre investigators to receive Human Rights Award," *National Catholic Reporter*, March 22, 2019, www.ncronline.org/news/quick-reads/el-mozote-massacre-investigators-receive-human-rights-award
10 As Ray Bonner noted, martyrdom is the final step before sainthood. Ibid., Raymond Bonner, 2016.
11 Jon Lee Anderson, "Archbishop Óscar Romero Becomes a Saint, But His Death Still Haunts El Salvador," *New Yorker*, October 22, 2018, www.newyorker.com/news/daily-comment/archbishop-oscar-romero-becomes-a-saint-but-his-death-still-haunts-el-salvador
12 Ibid., Jon Lee Anderson, 2018.
13 C-SPAN, "Southern Border Troop Deployment," January 29, 2019, www.c-span.org/video/?457334-1/defense-department-officials-testify-military-support-southern-border&start=3830. At the hearing, one congressman also noted that it cost $11 billion to shut the government down.
14 Damian Paletta and Eric Werner, "Trump to Demand 8.6 Billion in New Wall Funding, Setting up Fresh Battle with Congress," *Washington Post*, March 10, 2019, www.washingtonpost.com/business/economy/trump-to-demand-86-billion-in-new-wall-funding-setting-up-fresh-battle-with-congress/2019/03/10/c5eec1e6-4342-11e9-90f0-0ccfeec87a61_story.html?utm_term=.a55148ed770c
15 Jake Johnson, "Bernie Sanders Says Trump's Budget is 'Breathtaking in its Degree of Cruelty' with Trillions in Safety Net Cuts," *Alternet.org*, March 11, 2019, www.alternet.org/2019/03/bernie-sanders-says-trump-budget-is-breathtaking-in-its-degree-of-cruelty-with-trillions-in-safety-net-cuts/

16 Such reporting was a welcome turn from the way Republican Tax cuts were presented in mainstream media's neutral, analytical minutia, and even positive language, obscuring the overall effects that such a transfer of wealth would have on average Americans and economic justice in general.

17 As part of the United Nation's structure, the mission of the World Bank is to end poverty. However it is also mandated to help developing countries through financing investment and "mobilizing capital in international financial markets." According to its Articles of Agreement, policy decisions prioritize the facilitation of Capital investment and international trade. See Robin Andersen, "Conclusion," in *Routledge Companion to Media and Humanitarian Action*, ed. Robin Andersen and Purnaka L. de Silva (New York: Routledge, 2018).

18 Amnesty International, "Honduras: Government deploys dangerous and Illegal Tactics to Silence Population," December 8, 2017, www. amnesty.org/en/latest/news/2017/12/honduras-government-deploys-dangerous-and-illegal-tactics-to-silence-population/

19 Marta Martinez, "Impunity's Eclipse: The Long Journey to the Historic Genocide Trial in Guatemala," *The International Center for Transitional Justice* (ICTJ), www.ictj.org/sites/default/files/subsites/guatemala-genocide-impunity-eclipse/

20 Pedro Portal, "Immigrant and Community Leaders Rally Asking for the Shut Down of the Homestead Detention Center," *Miami Herald*, March 5, 2019, www.miamiherald.com/news/local/immigration/article 227159909.html

21 Tracy Jan, "Banks Bow to Pressure to Stop Profiting from Trump's Immigration Policy, But Big Tech Remains Defiant," *Washington Post*, March 10 2019, www.washingtonpost.com/business/economy/banks-bow-to-pressure-to-stop-profiting-from-trumps-immigration-policy-but-big-tech-remains-defiant/2019/03/10/87bec704-40ea-11e9-a0d3-1210e58a94cf_story.html?utm_term=.07d58282d8e1&wpisrc=nl_politics&wpmm=1

22 Robin Andersen, *A Century of Media, A Century of War* (New York: Peter Lang, 2006).

23 Tom Jones, Mari Payton, and Bill Feather, "Source: Leaked Documents Show the U.S. Government Tracking Journalists and Immigration Advocates Through a Secret Database," *7 Investigates*, NBC, March 6, 2019, www.nbcsandiego.com/investigations/Source-Leaked-Documents-Show-the-US-Government-Tracking-Journalists-and-Advocates-Through-a-Secret-Database-506783231.html

24 Eion Higgins, "'Outrageous Violation of First Amendment': Leaked Docs Reveal Trump Tracked Journalists and Rights Advocate at Border," *Common Dreams*, March 7, 2019, www.commondreams.org/news/2019/03/07/outrageous-violation-first-amendment-leaked-docs-reveal-trump-tracked-journalists?cd-origin=rss&utm_term=%27Outrageous%20Violation%20of%20First%20Amendment%27%3A%20Leaked%20Docs%20Reveal%20Trump%20Tracked%20Journalists%20and%20Rights%20Advocates%20at%20Border&utm_campaign=Progressive%20Democrats%20Condemn%20US-Backed%20Regime%20Change%20in%20Venezuela%20%7C%20News%20%2526%20Views&utm_content=email&utm_source=Daily%20

Newsletter&utm_medium=Email&cm_mmc=Act-On%20Software-_-email-_-Progressive%20Democrats%20Condemn%20US-Backed%20Regime%20Change%20in%20Venezuela%20%7C%20News%20%2526%20Views-_-%27Outrageous%20Violation%20of%20First%20Amendment%27%3A%20Leaked%20Docs%20Reveal%20Trump%20Tracked%20Journalists%20and%20Rights%20Advocates%20at%20

25 Salvador Hernandez, "The US Compiled a Secret List of Journalists, Attorneys, and Activists to Question At Border," BuzzFeed News, March 7, 2019, www.buzzfeednews.com/article/salvadorhernandez/government-list-journalists-border-immigration-question

26 Ibid., Tom Jones, Mari Payton, and Bill Feather, 2019.

27 Natasha Bertrand, "Top Trump Lawyer in Private Email Exchange: Me and Kelly are the Adults in the Room," *Business Insider*, September 6, 2017, www.businessinsider.com/trump-lawyer-ty-cobb-email-russia-2017-9

28 Monica Hess wrote a commentary for the *Washington Post* titled, "John Kelly and the Myth of the Adult in the Room," December 10, 2018, www.syracuse.com/opinion/2018/12/john_kelly_and_the_myth_of_the_adult_in_the_room_commentary.html

29 John Burnett, "Transcript: White House Chief of Staff John Kelly's Interview with NPR," NPR, May 11, 2018, www.npr.org/2018/05/11/610116389/transcript-white-house-chief-of-staff-john-kellys-interview-with-npr

30 Hayley Miller, "John Kelly Blames Jeff Sessions for Family Separation Policy: 'He Surprised Us'," *Huffington Post*, December 30, 2018, www.huffingtonpost.com/entry/john-kelly-jeff-sessions-family-separation_us_5c28d01ae4b08aaf7a917c37?utm_medium=email&utm_campaign=__TheMorningEmail__123118&utm_content=__TheMorningEmail__123118+CID_b2f0ff2bc32a82d2892d9768a1ab-f9c3&utm_source=Email%20marketing%20software&utm_term=HuffPost&ncid=newsltushpmgnews__TheMorningEmail__123118

31 Jake Johnston, "How Pentagon Official May Have Encouraged a 2009 Coup in Honduras," *The Intercept*, August 29, 2017, https://theintercept.com/2017/08/29/honduras-coup-us-defense-departmetnt-center-hemispheric-defense-studies-chds/

32 Ibid., Jake Johnston 2017. In her 2018 book, *The Long Honduran Night*, Dana Frank includes a photograph of John Kelly and Juan Orlando Hernández standing side by side, as visual documentation of their close relationship, which she details in the book.

33 Ibid., Hayley Miller, 2018.

34 Ibid., Raymond Bonner, 2016.

35 Ibid., Raymond Bonner, 2016.

36 Ibid., Robin Andersen, 2006.

37 Tom Gallagher, "San Francisco democratic Adopt Venezuela Stance Diametrically Opposed to Pelosi's," *Common Dreams*, March 12, 2019, www.commondreams.org/views/2019/03/12/san-francisco-democrats-adopt-venezuela-stance-diametrically-opposed-pelosis

38 For an excellent discussion of U.S. attempts to destabilize Venezuela, and the loss of a historical frame able to understand the role of "Chavismo," see Steve Striffler, "Venezuela, US Solidarity, and the Future of Socialism," *Portside*, March 26, 2019, https://portside.org/2019-03-26/venezuela-us-solidarity-and-future-socialism

39 Ibid, Tom Gallagher, 2019.

40 Ibid, Tom Gallagher, 2019.
41 *Global Witness*, "Defenders of the Earth," July 2017. www.globalwit ness.org/en/campaigns/environmental-activists/defenders-earth/
42 Glenn Greenwald, "Veteran NBC/MSNBC Journalist Blasts the Network for being Captive to the National Security State and Reflectively Pro-War to Stop Trump," *The Intercept*, January 3, 2019, https://theintercept. com/2019/01/03/veteran-nbcmsnbc-journalist-blasts-the-network-for-being-captive-to-the-national-security-state-and-reflexively-pro-war-to-stop-trump/
43 Ibid., Glenn Greenwald, 2019.
44 Ibid., Glenn Greenwald, 2019.
45 Ibid., Robin Andersen, 2006. See also Robin Andersen and Tanner Mirrlees, "Introduction: Media, Technology, and the Culture of Militarism: Watching, Playing and Resisting the War Society," *Democratic Communique* 26, no. 2 (2014), http://journals.fcla.edu/demcom/article/view/83940
46 See for example, Deepa Kumar and Arun Kundnani, "Imagining National Security: The CIA, Hollywood, and the War on Terror," *Democratic Communique* 26, no. 2 (2014), http://journals.fcla.edu/demcom/article/view/83940
47 Ibid., John Burnett, 2018.
48 Brianna Rennix, "What Democratic Get Wrong About Immigration," *In These Times*, 43, no. 4 (April 2019).
49 Ibid., Brianna Rennix, 2019, 29.
50 Ibid., Brianna Rennix, 2019, 28.
51 Cited in Ibid., Brianna Rennix, 2019, 28.
52 Ibid., Brianna Rennix, 2019, 28.

Index

Note: *Italic* page numbers refer to figures and page numbers followed by "n" denote endnotes.

Printed in the United States
by Baker & Taylor Publisher Services